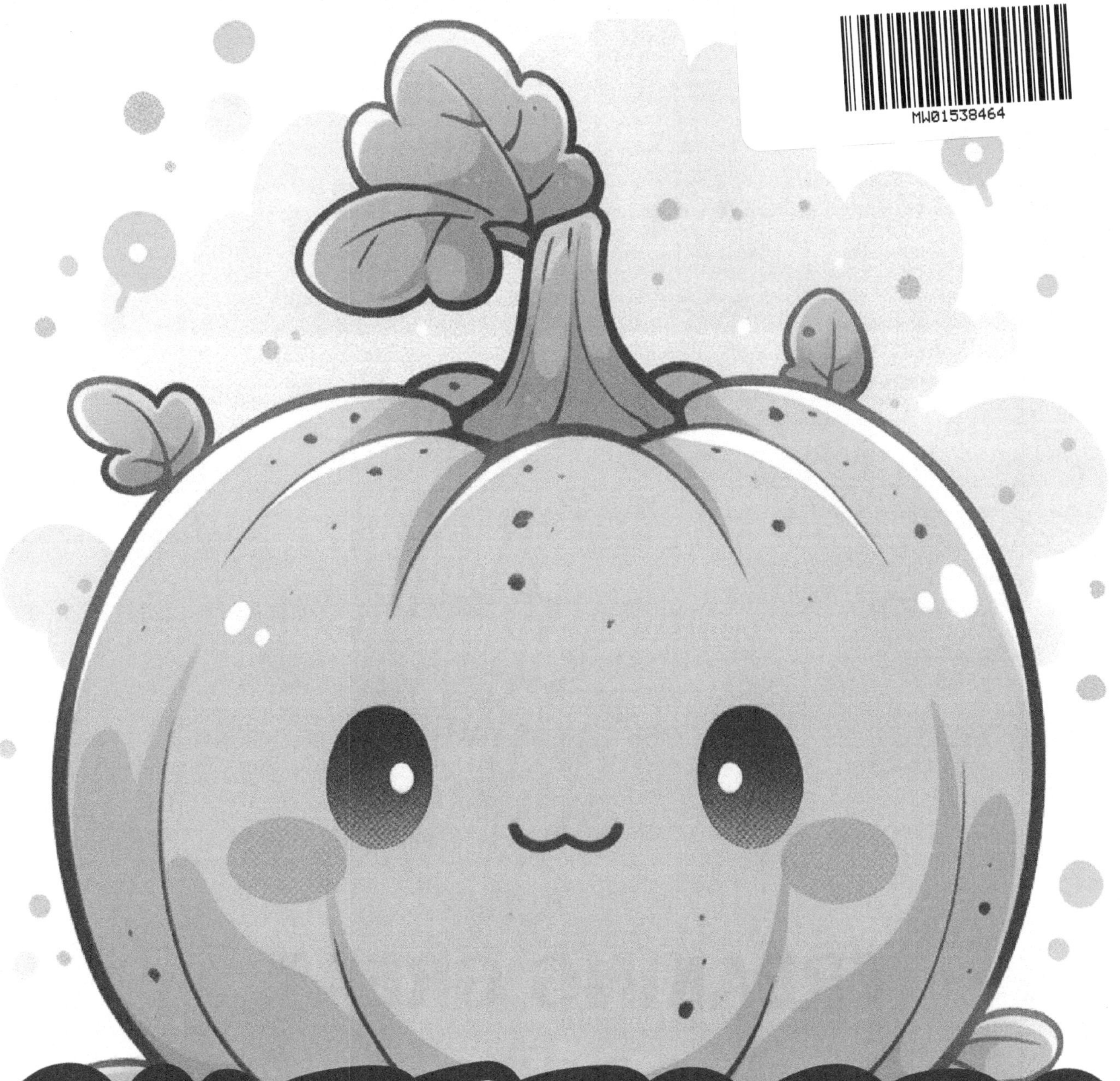

CUTETOPIA PUMPKINS

FREAKING GREAT BOOKS

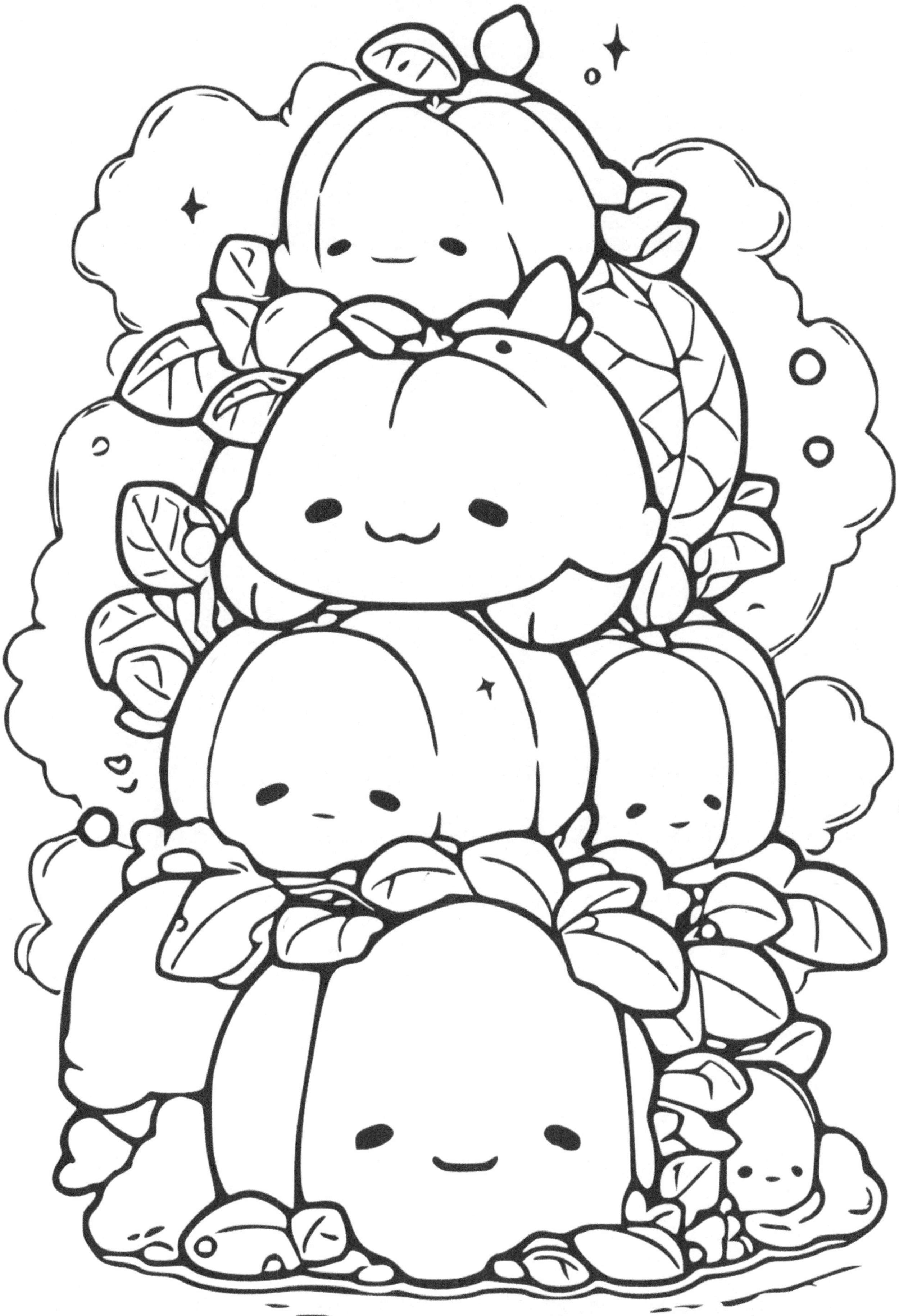

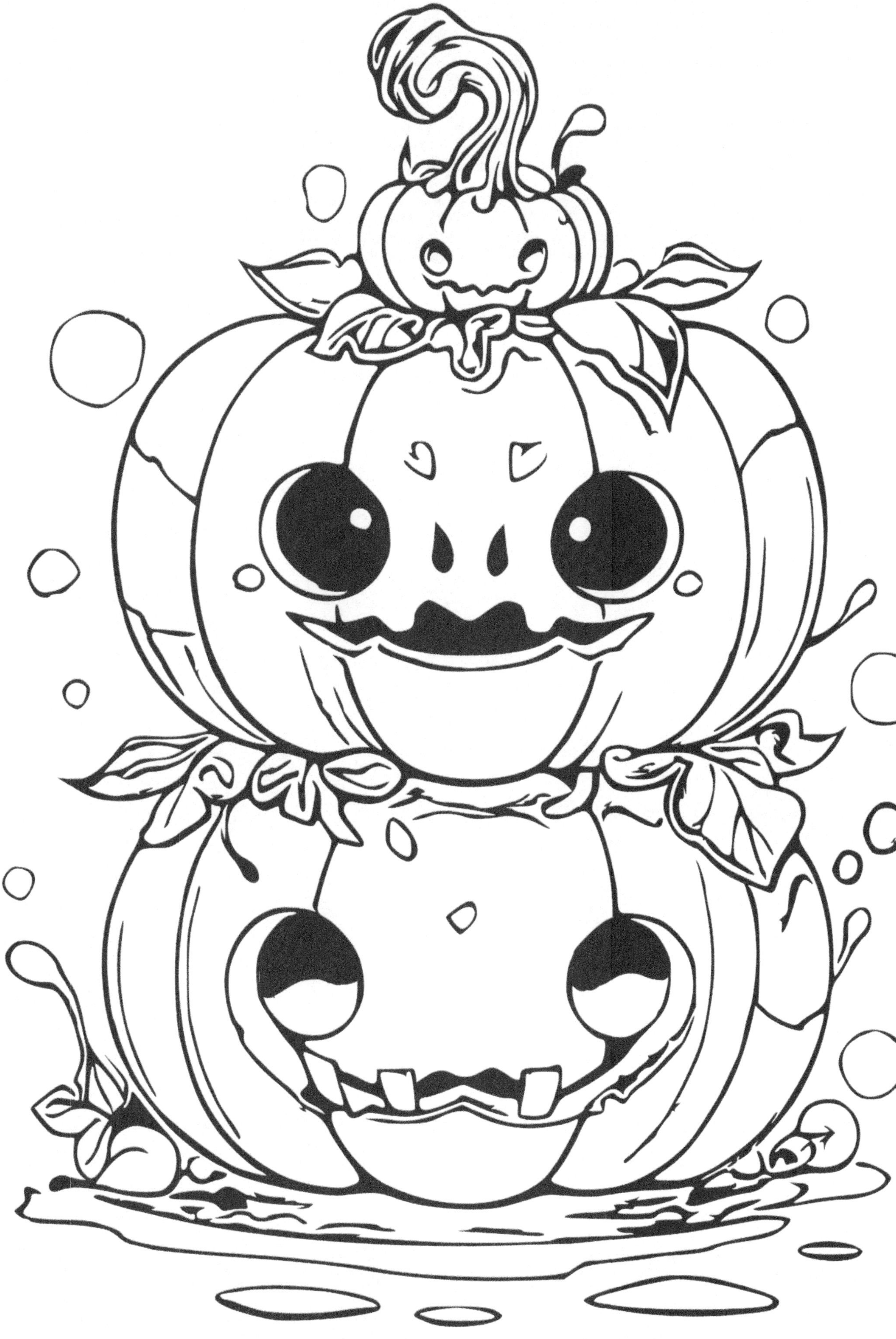

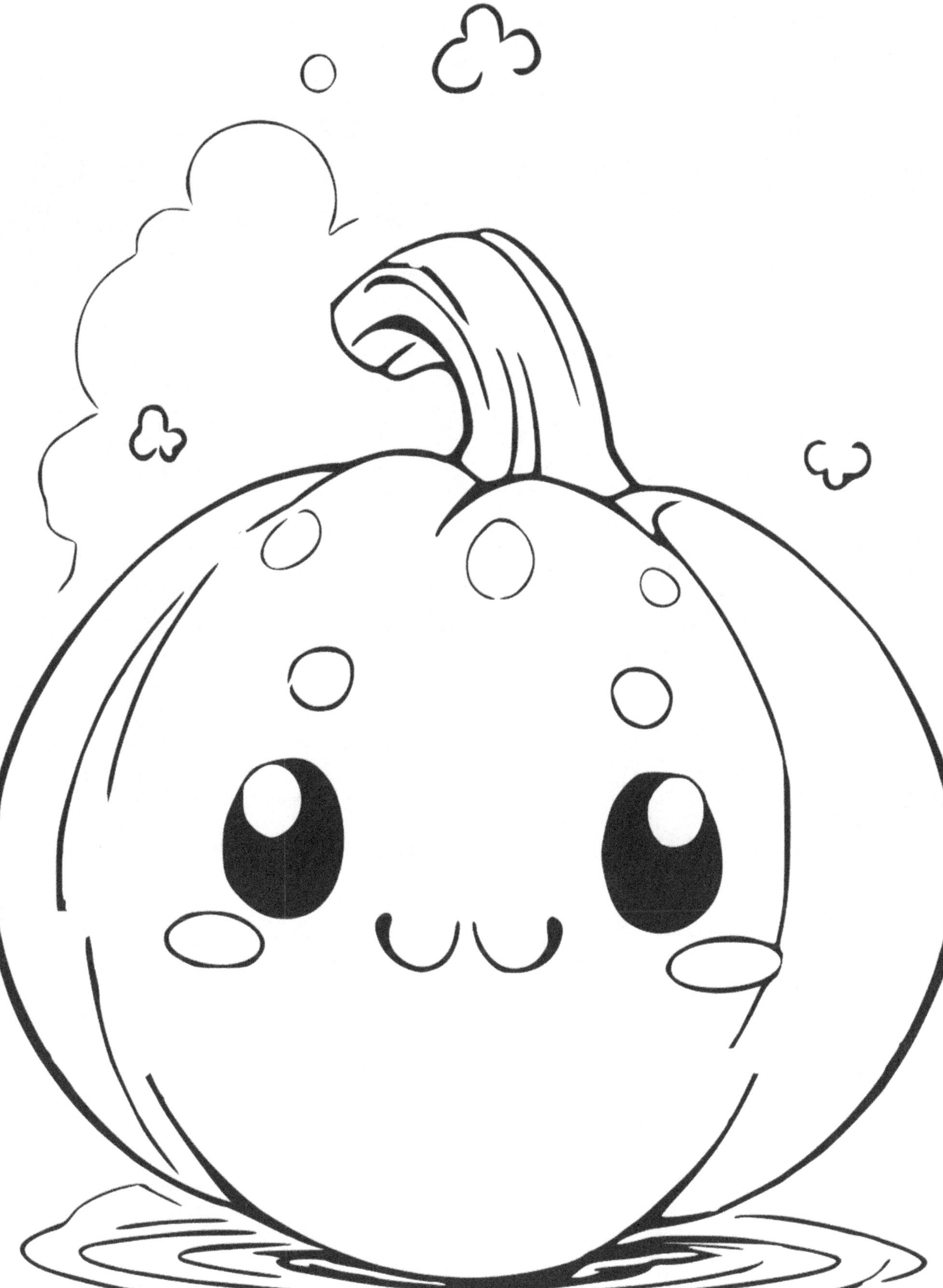

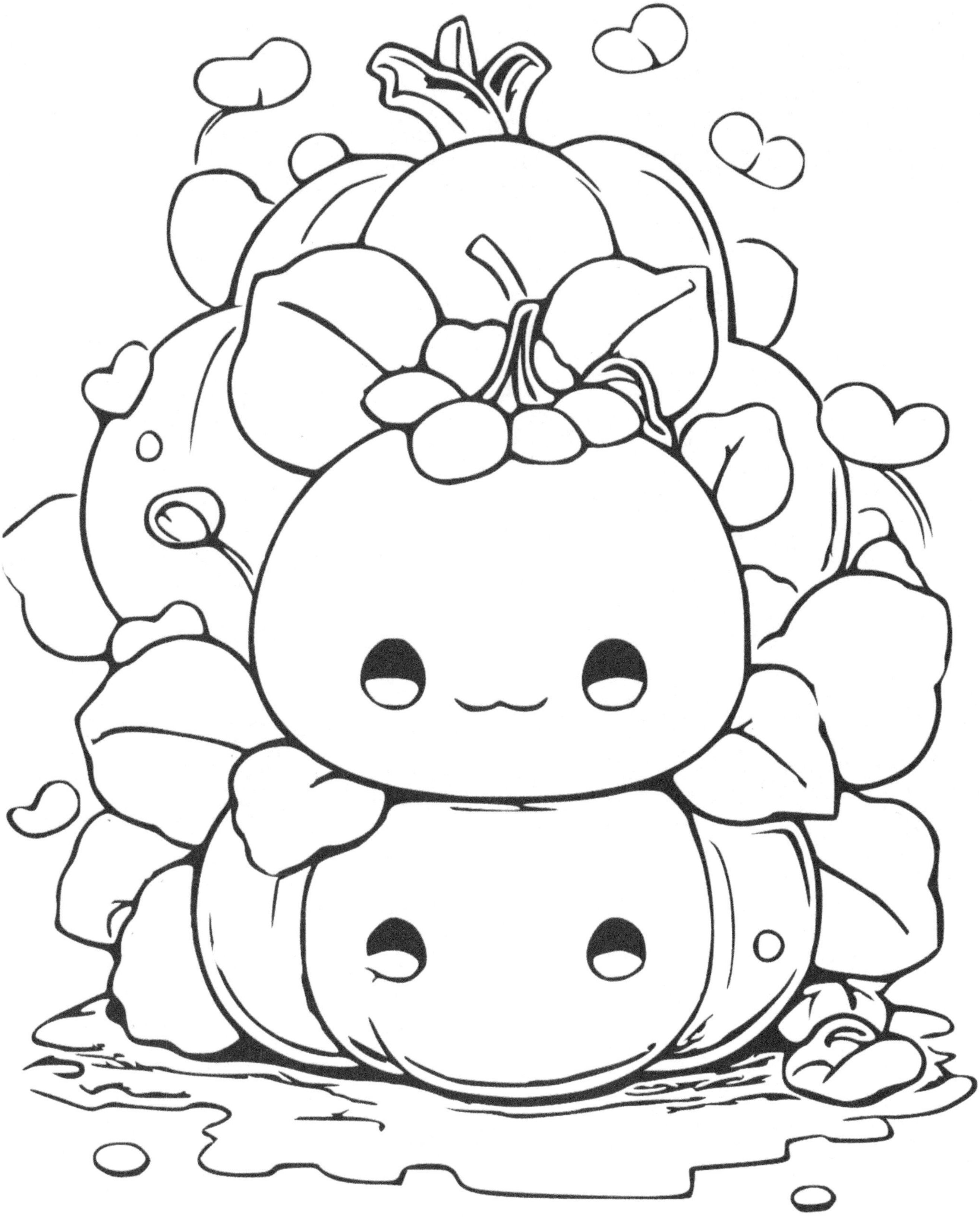

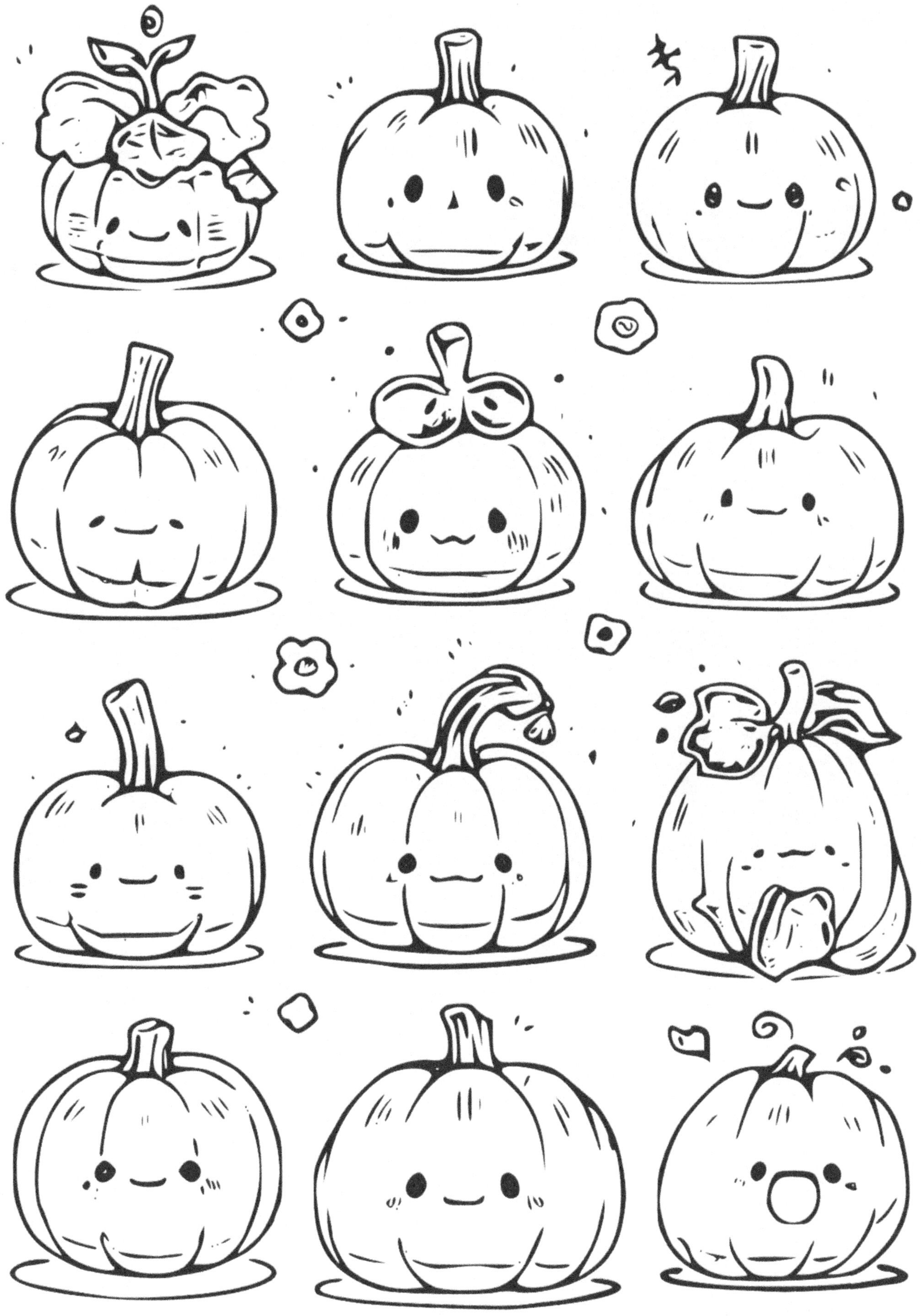

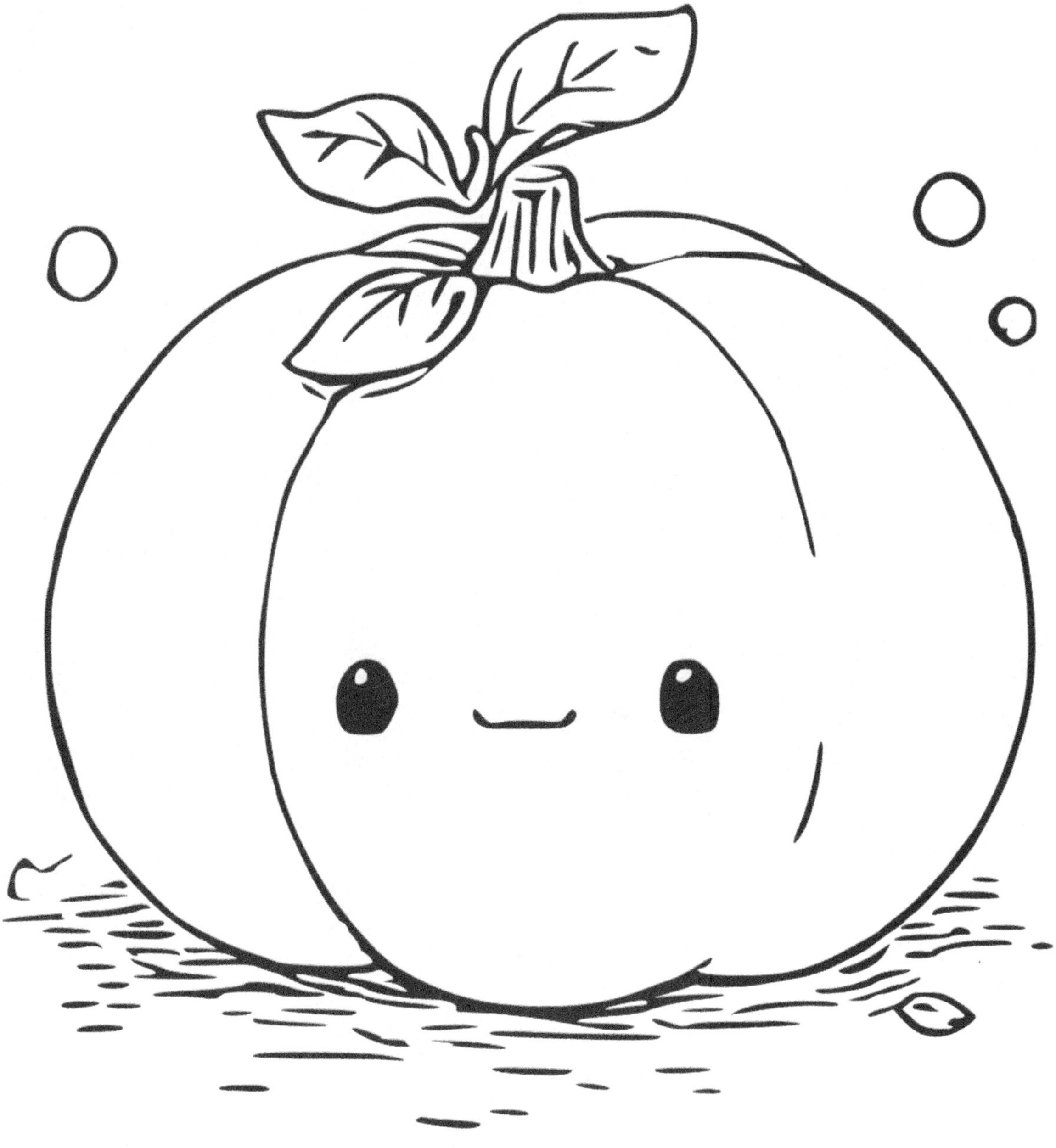

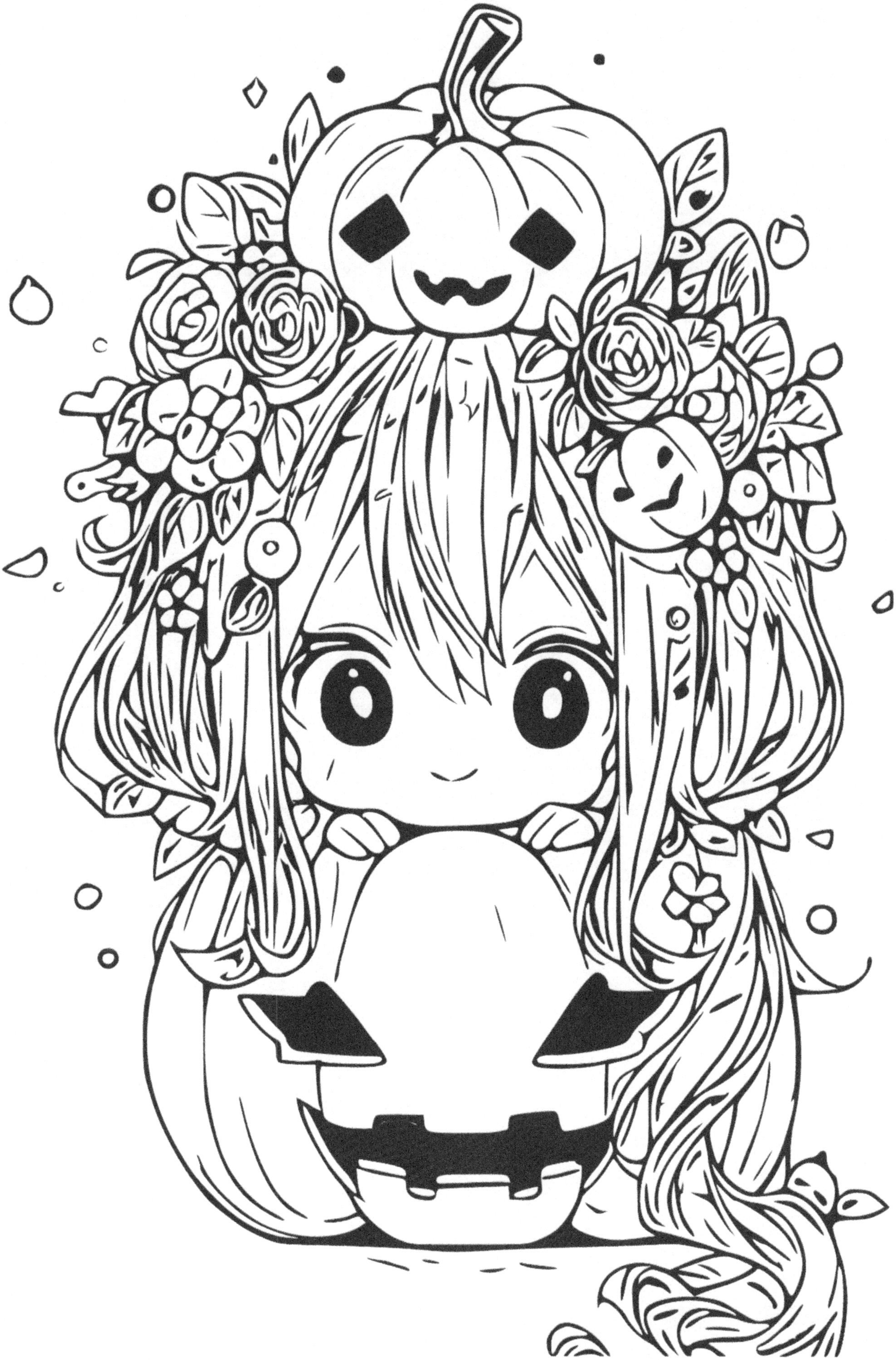

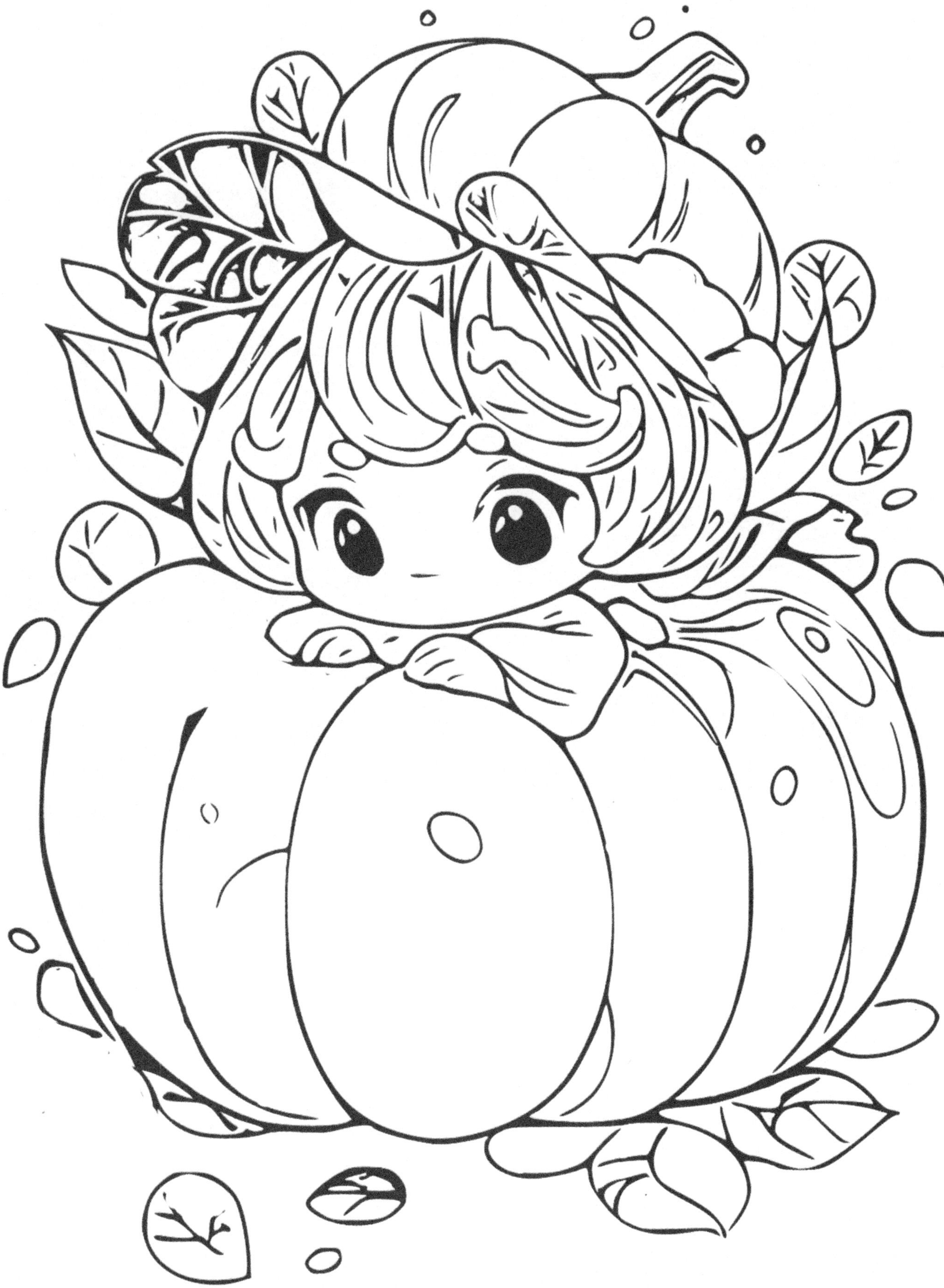

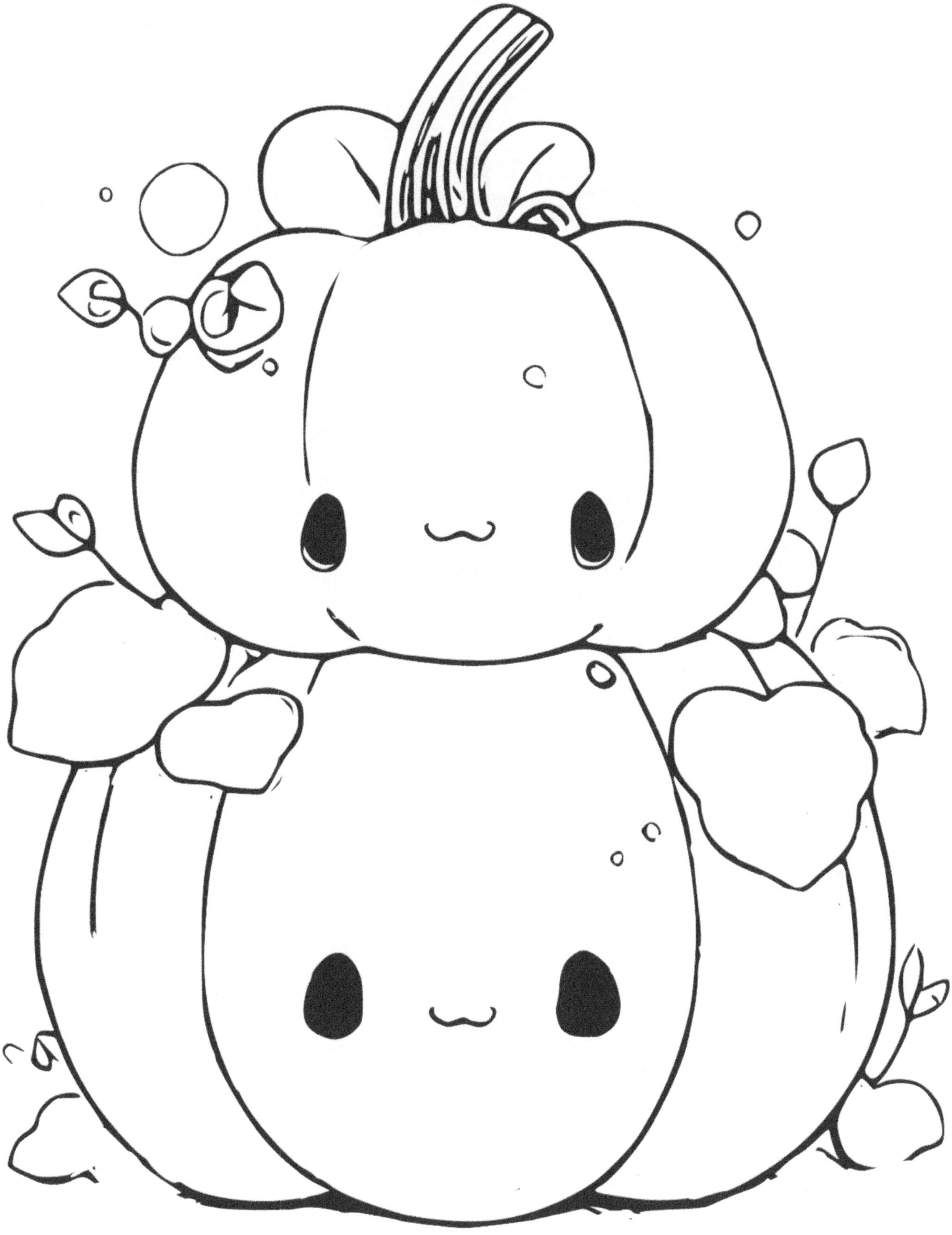

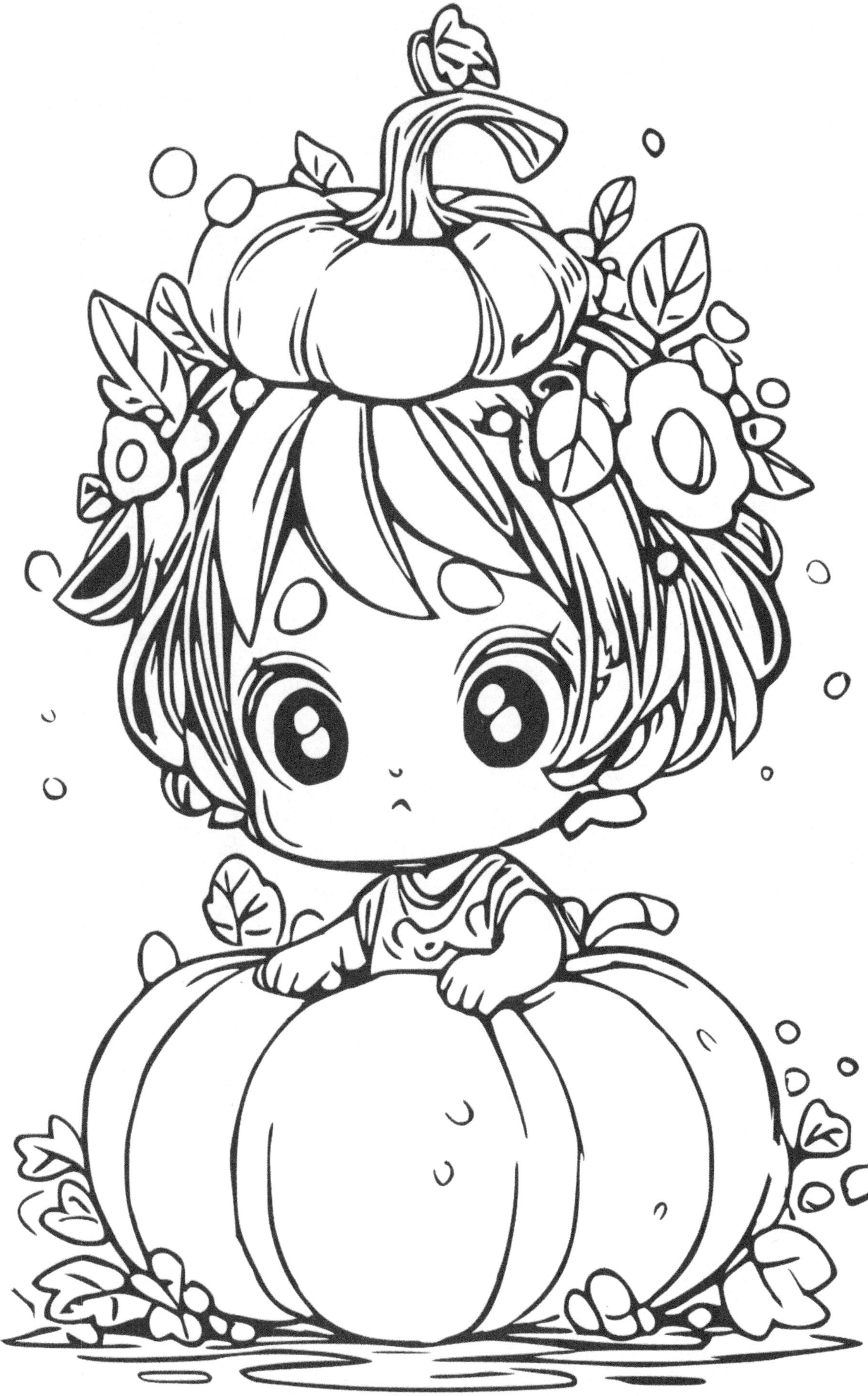

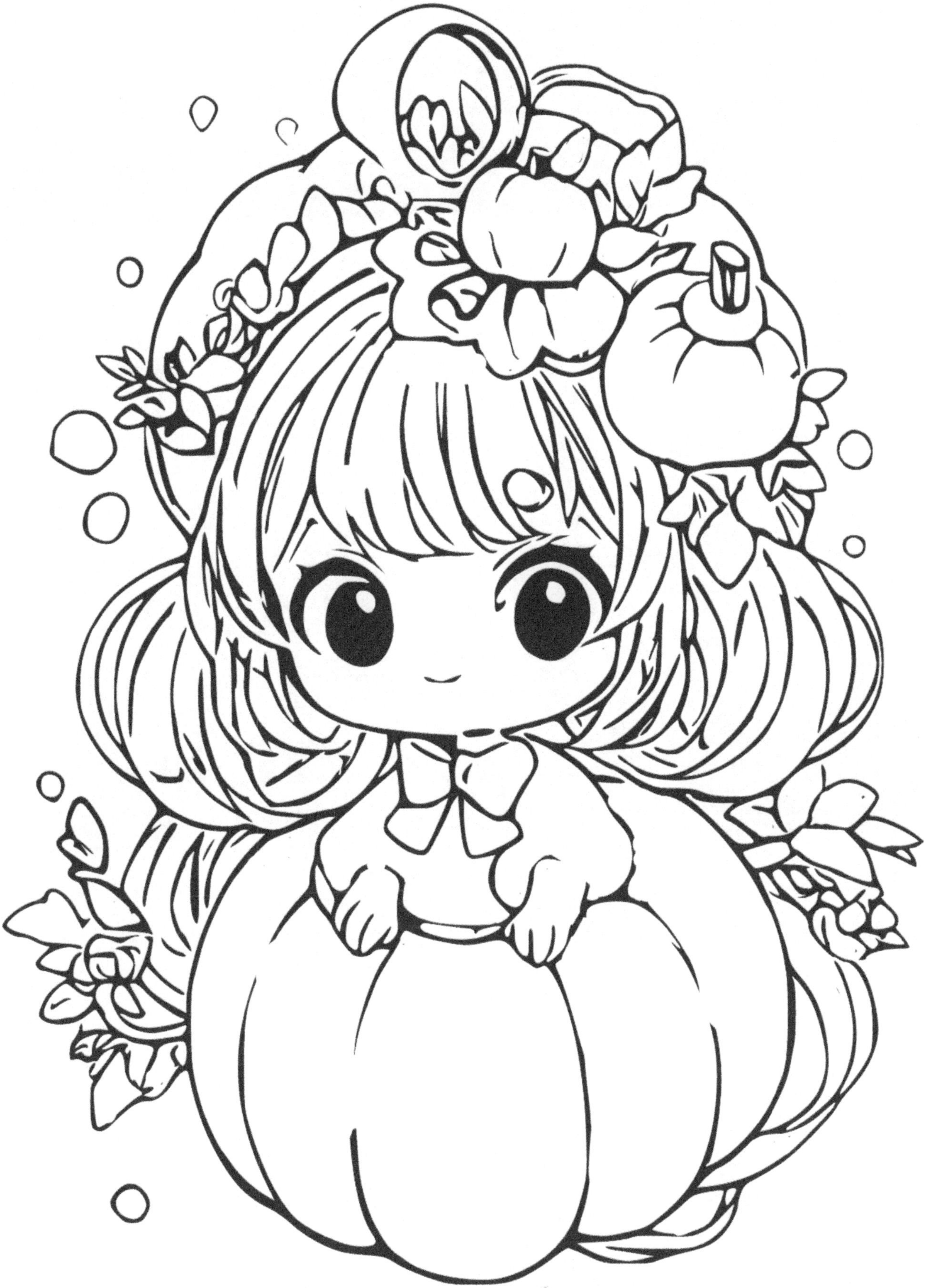

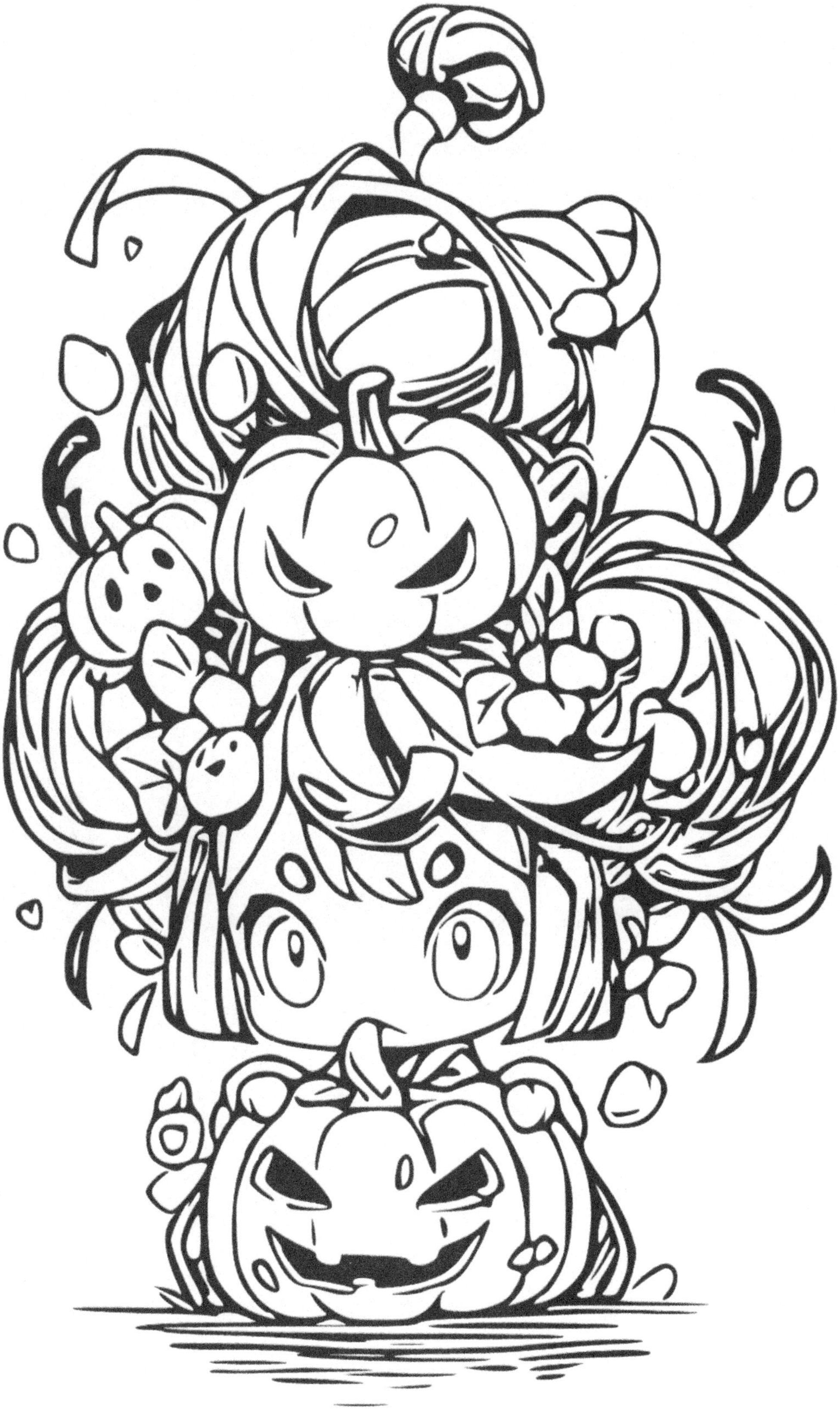

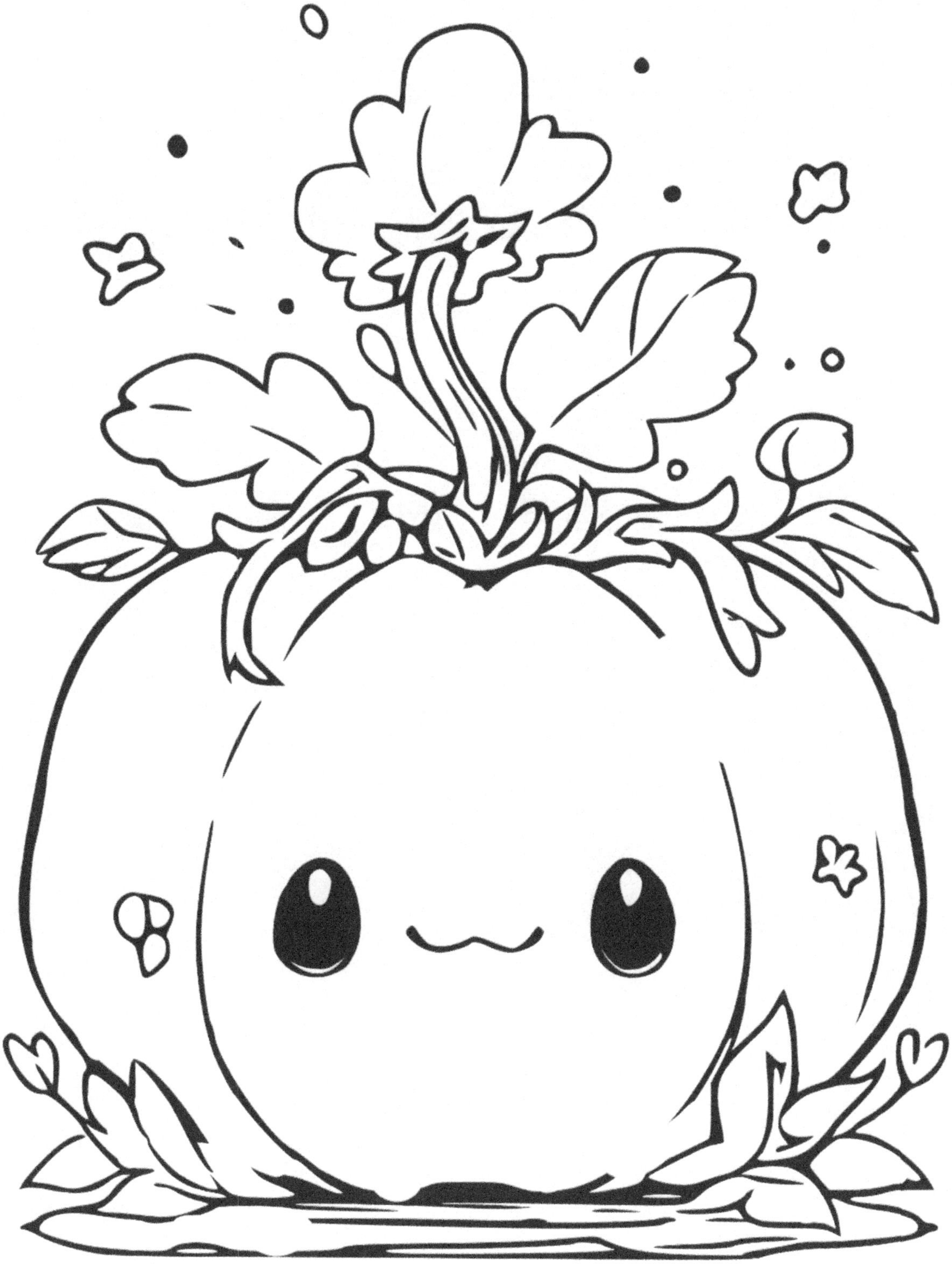

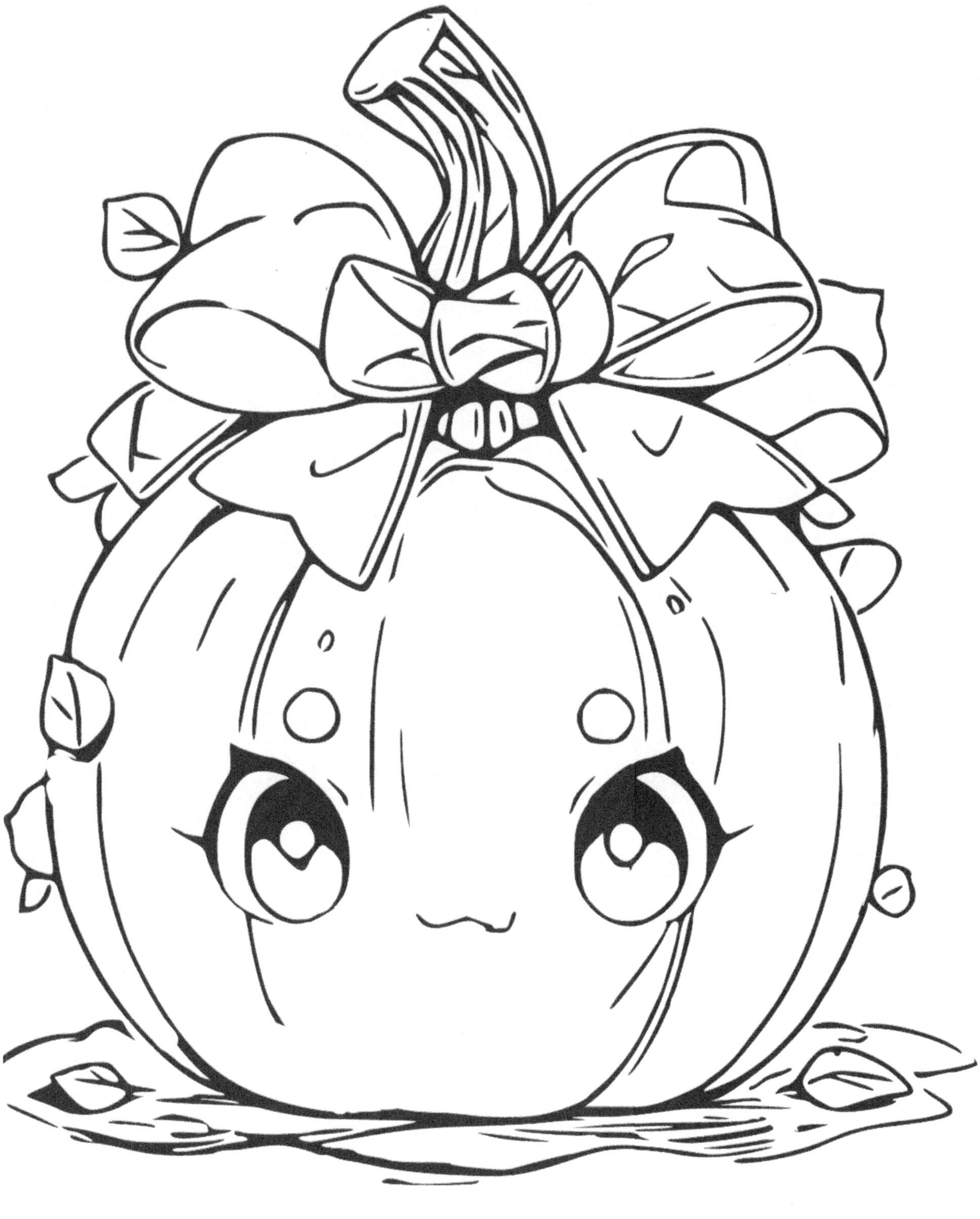

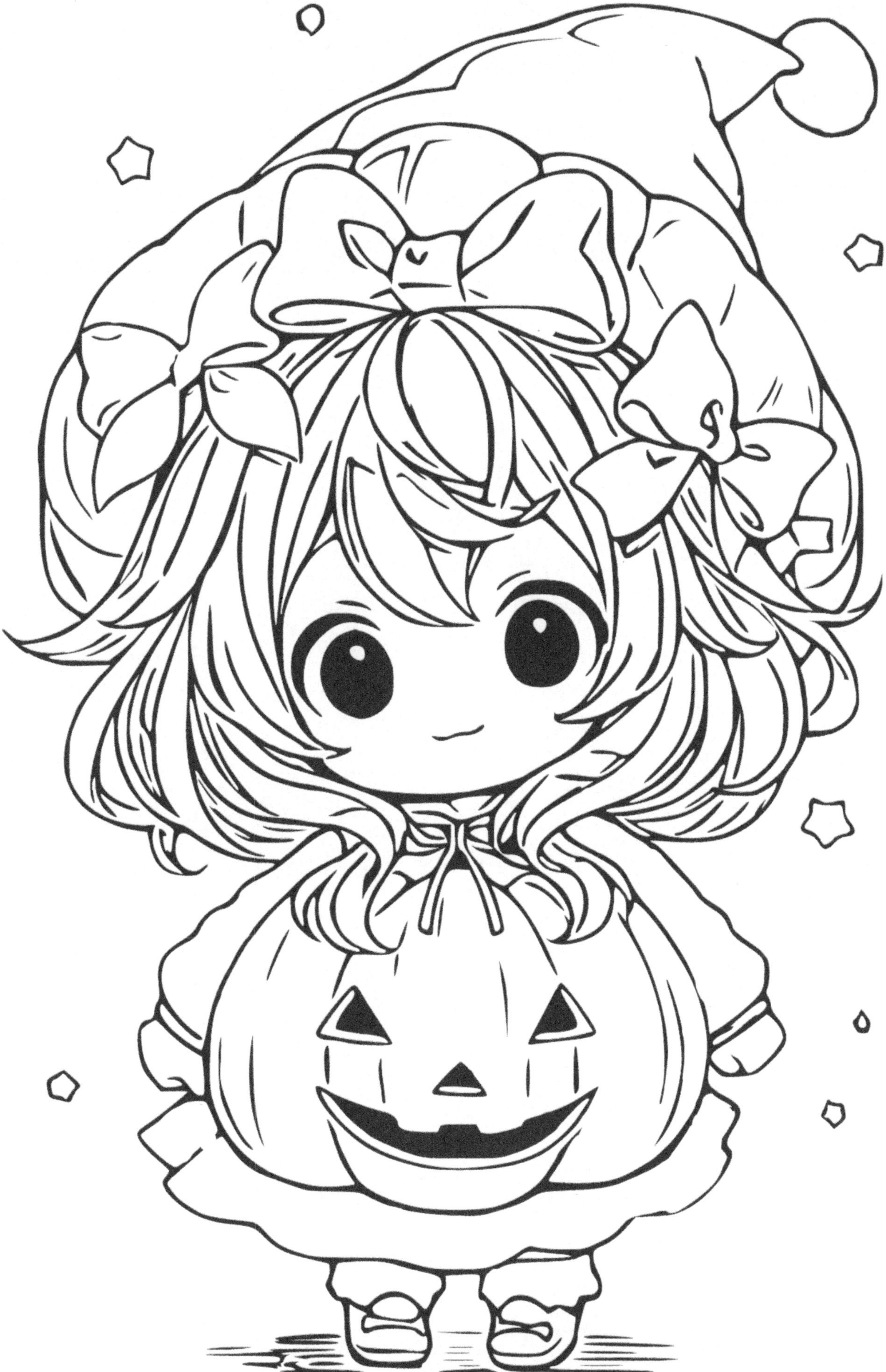

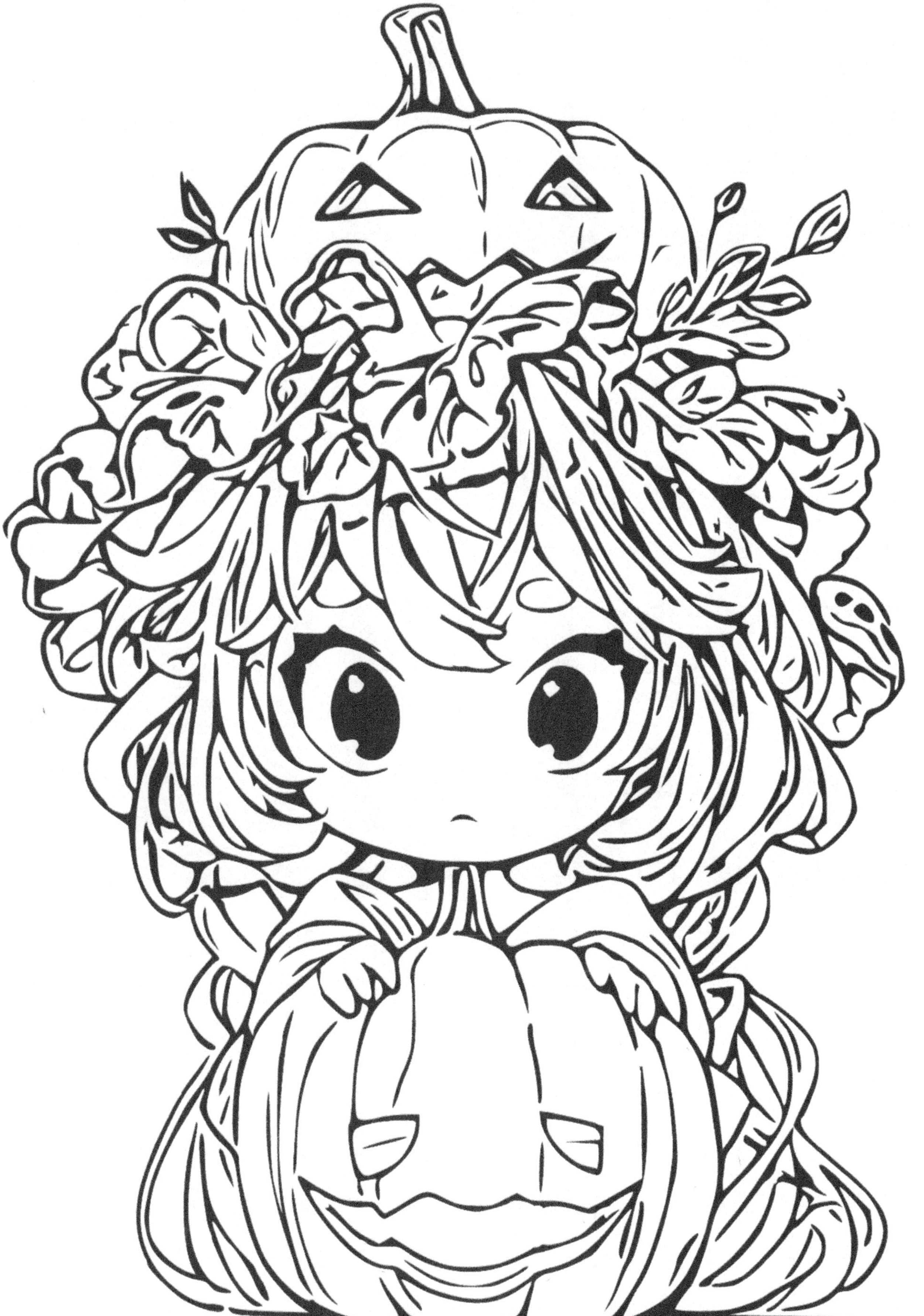

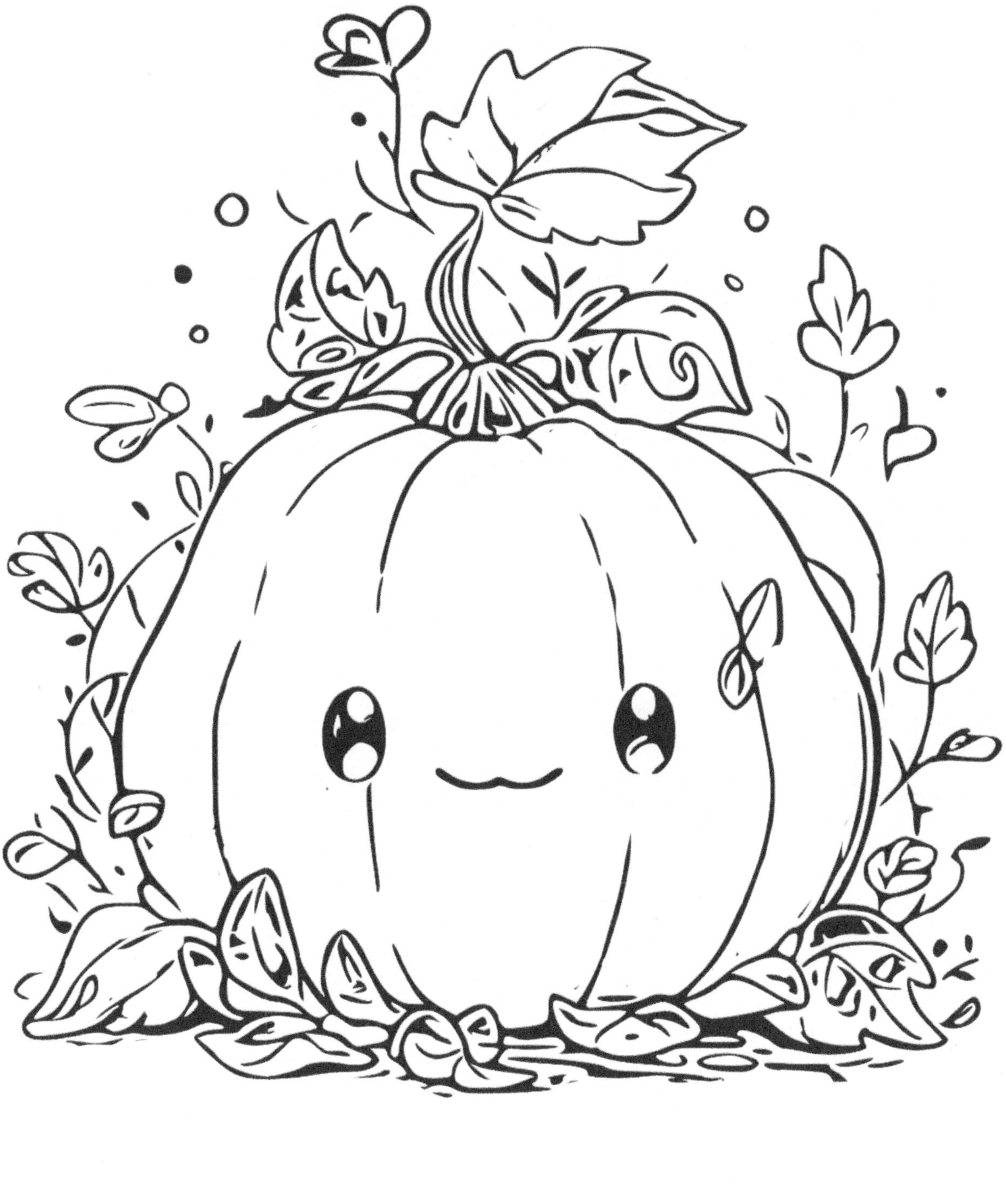

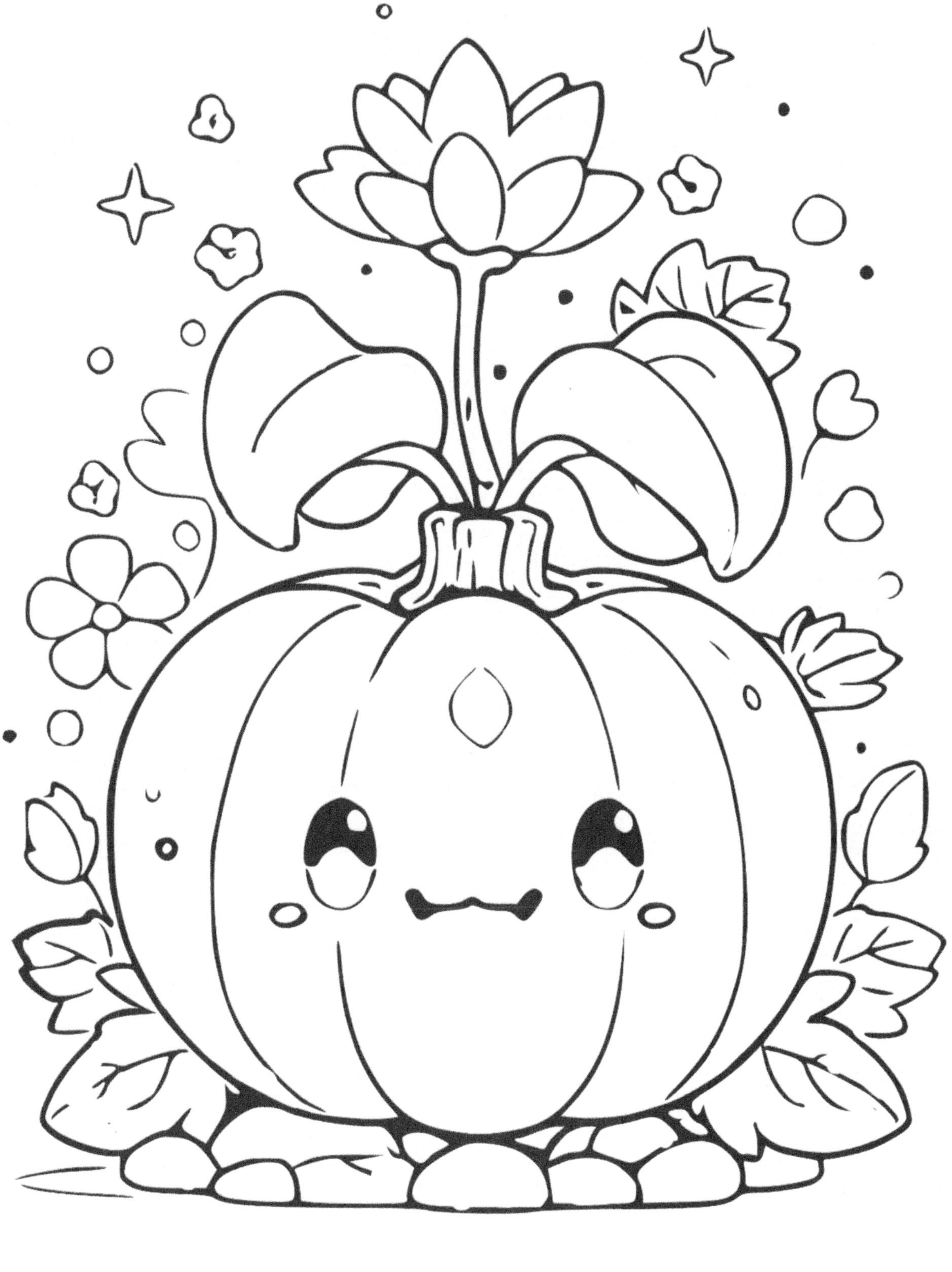

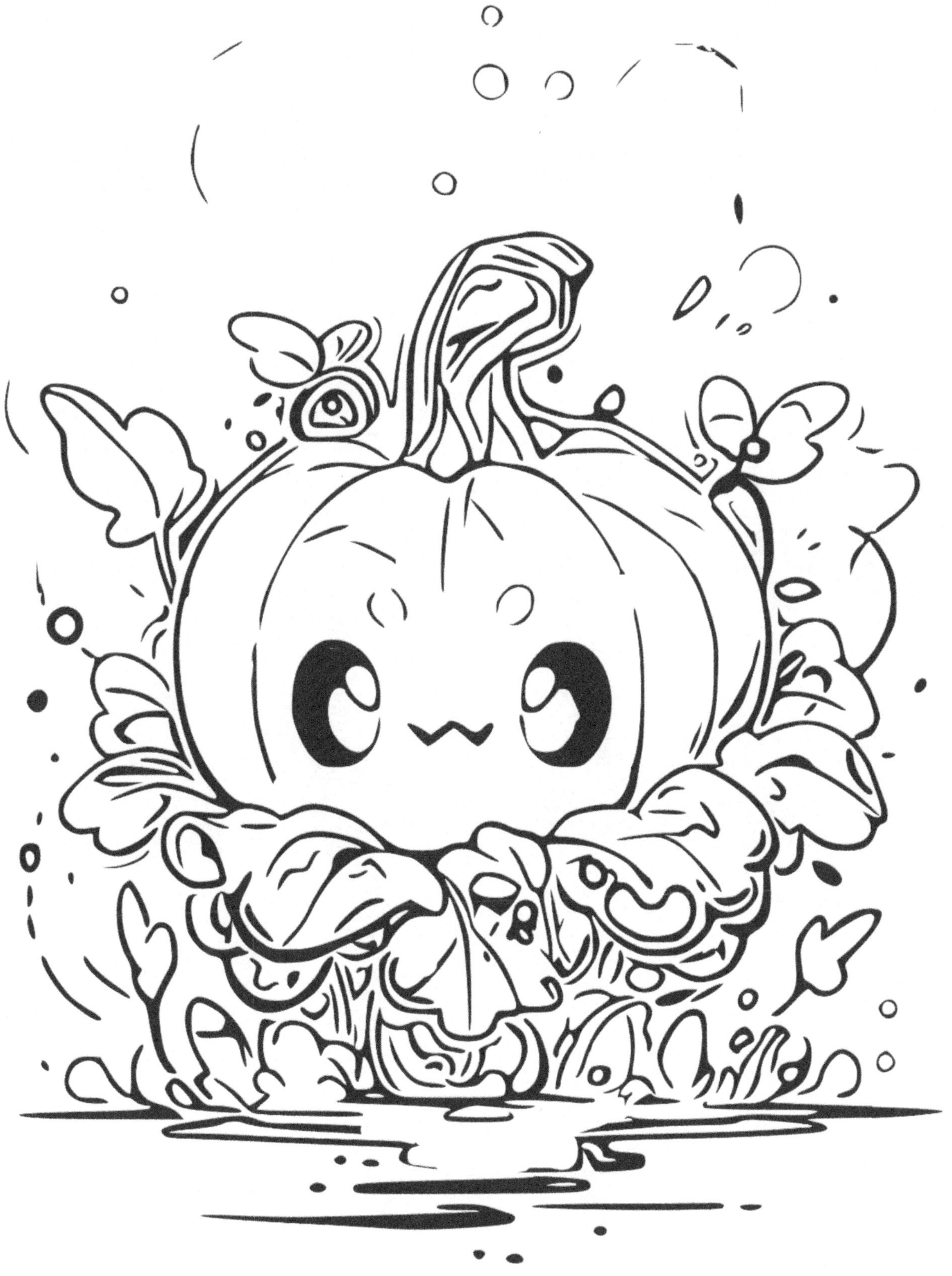

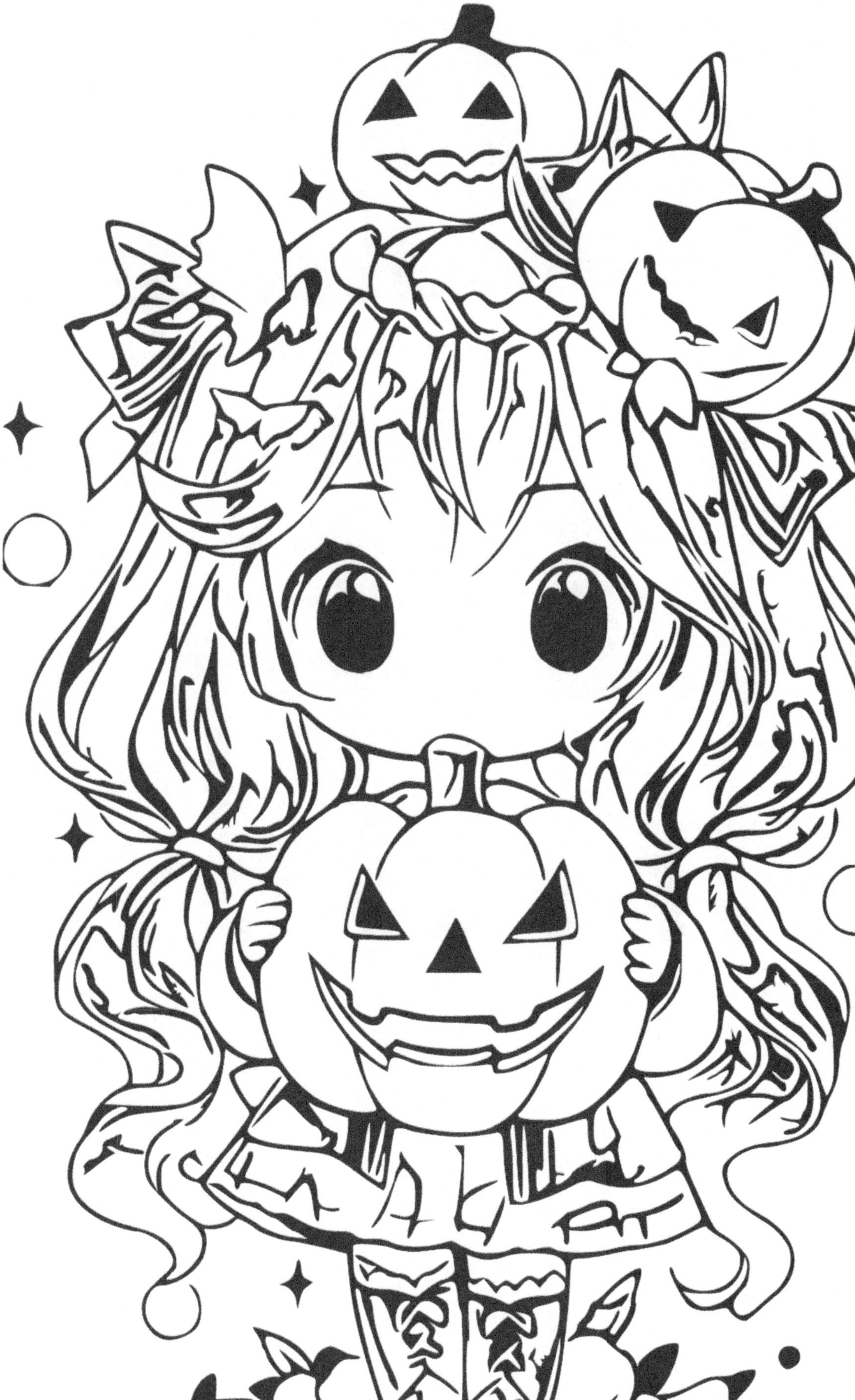

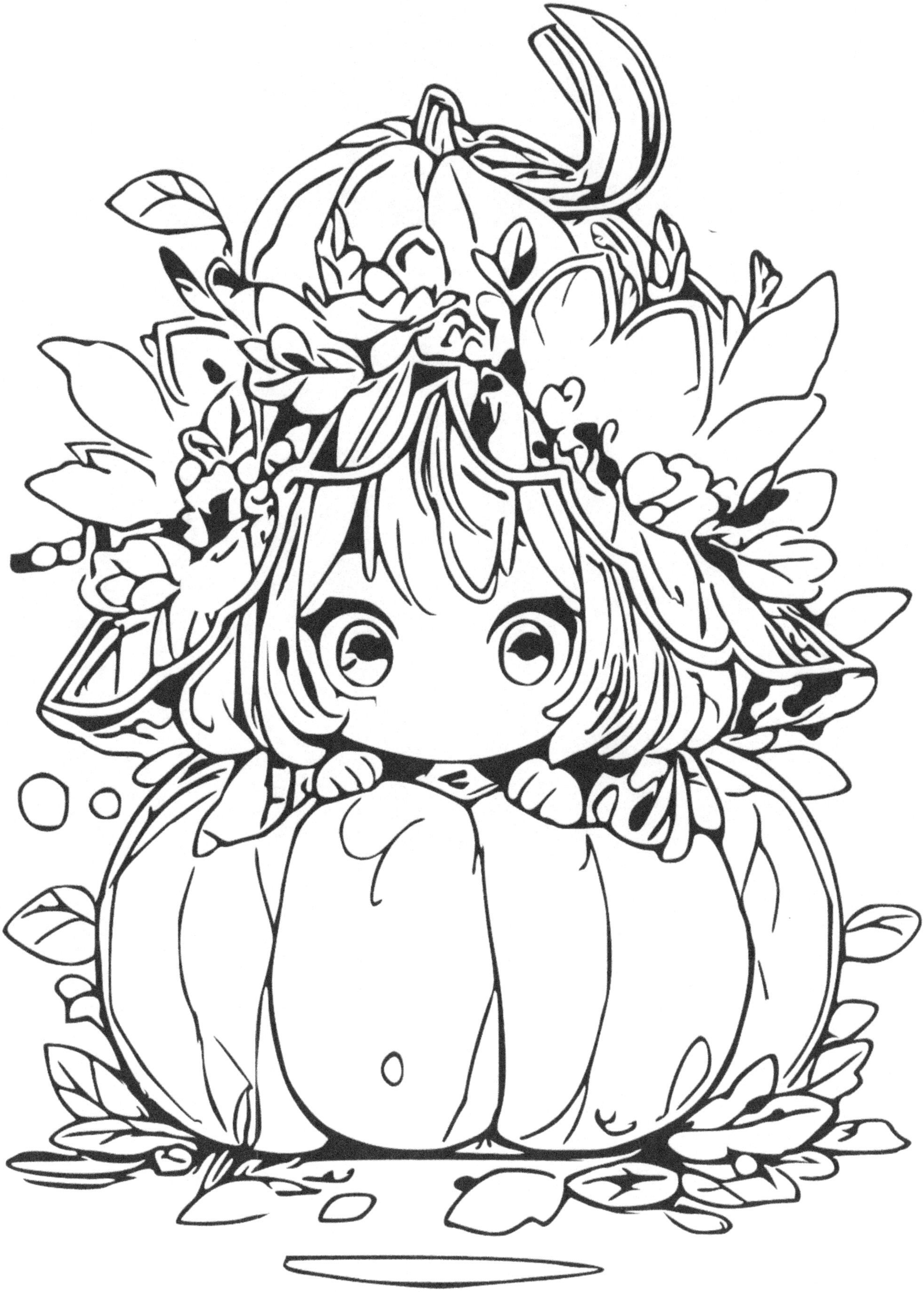

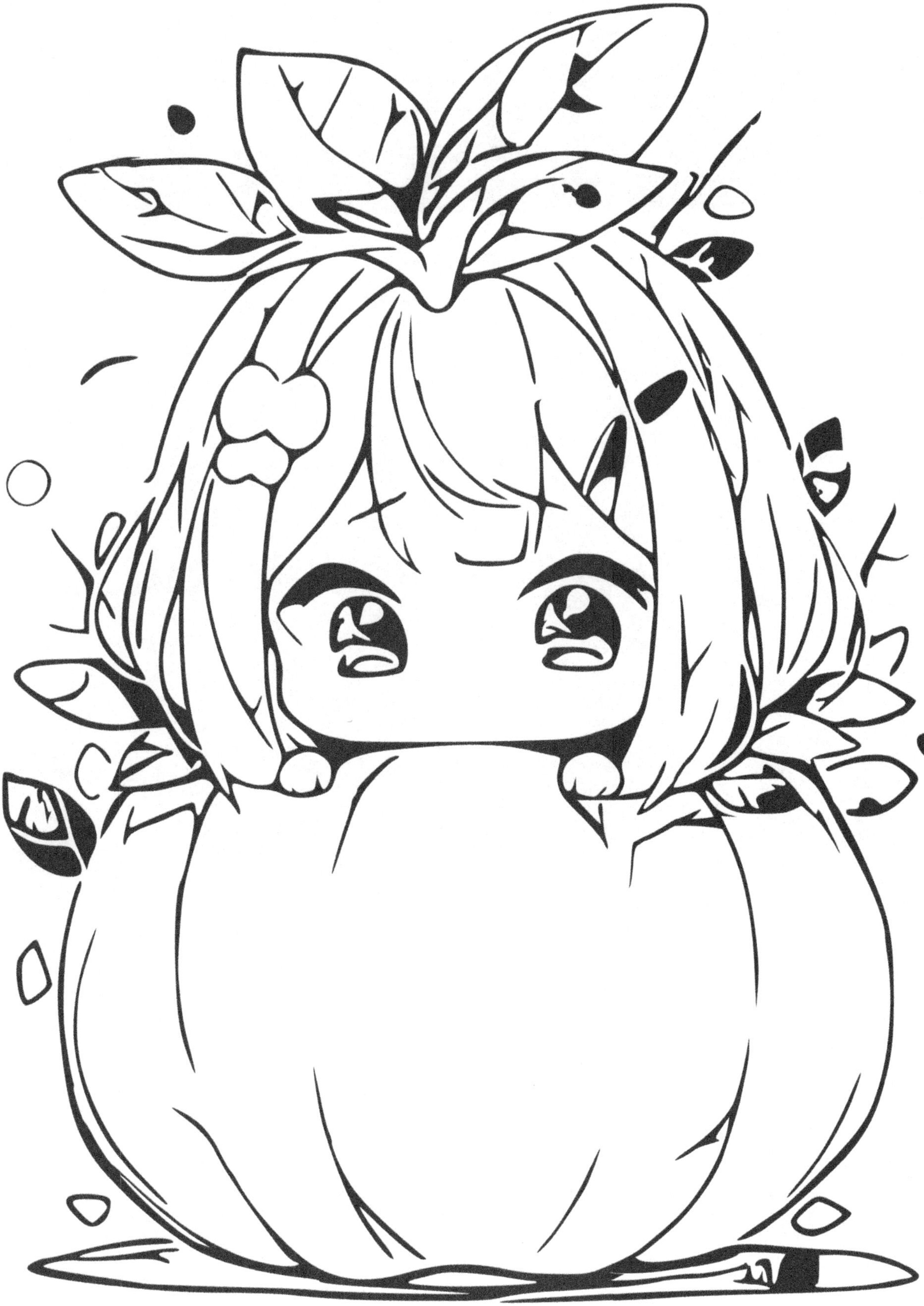

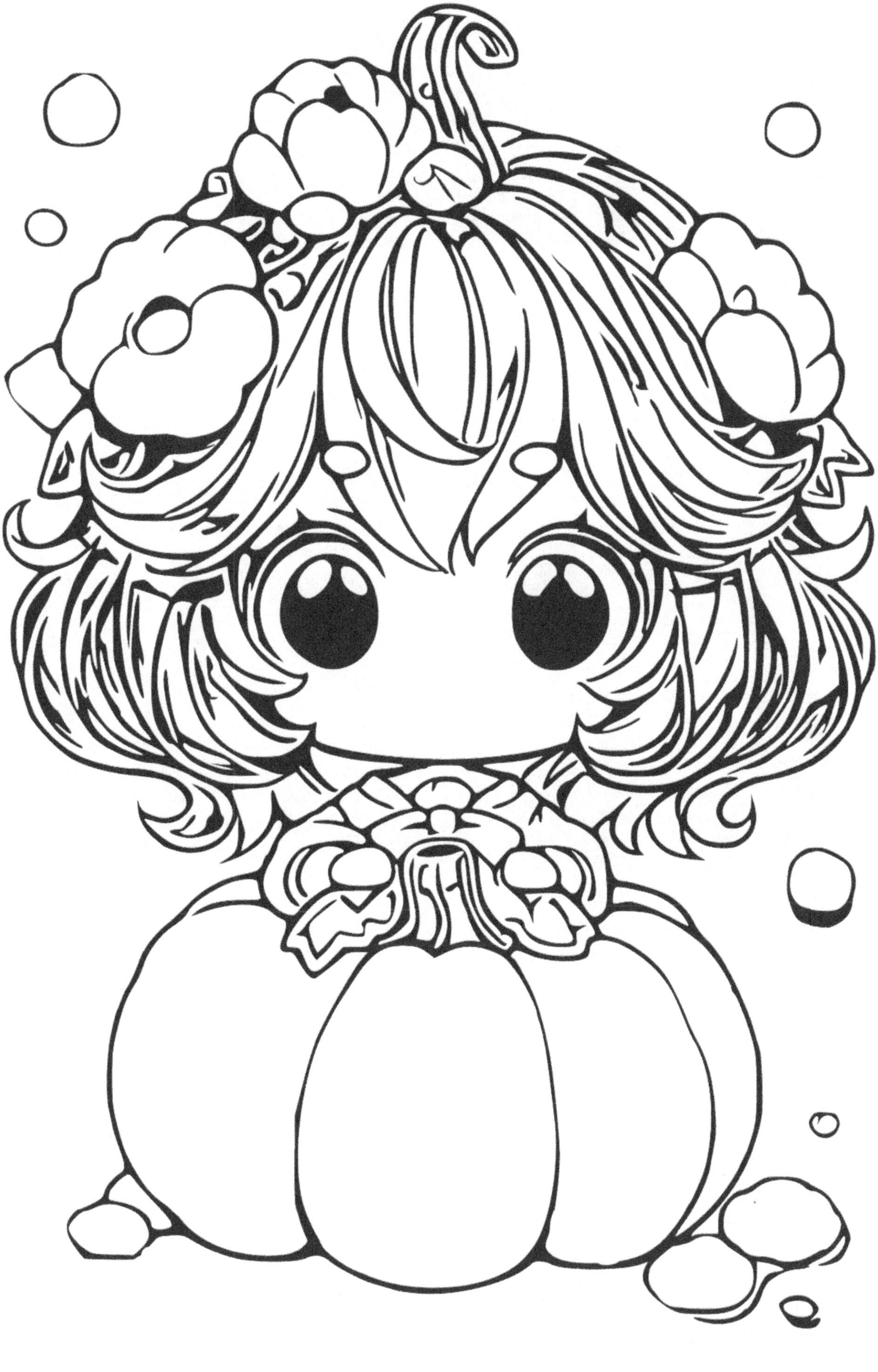

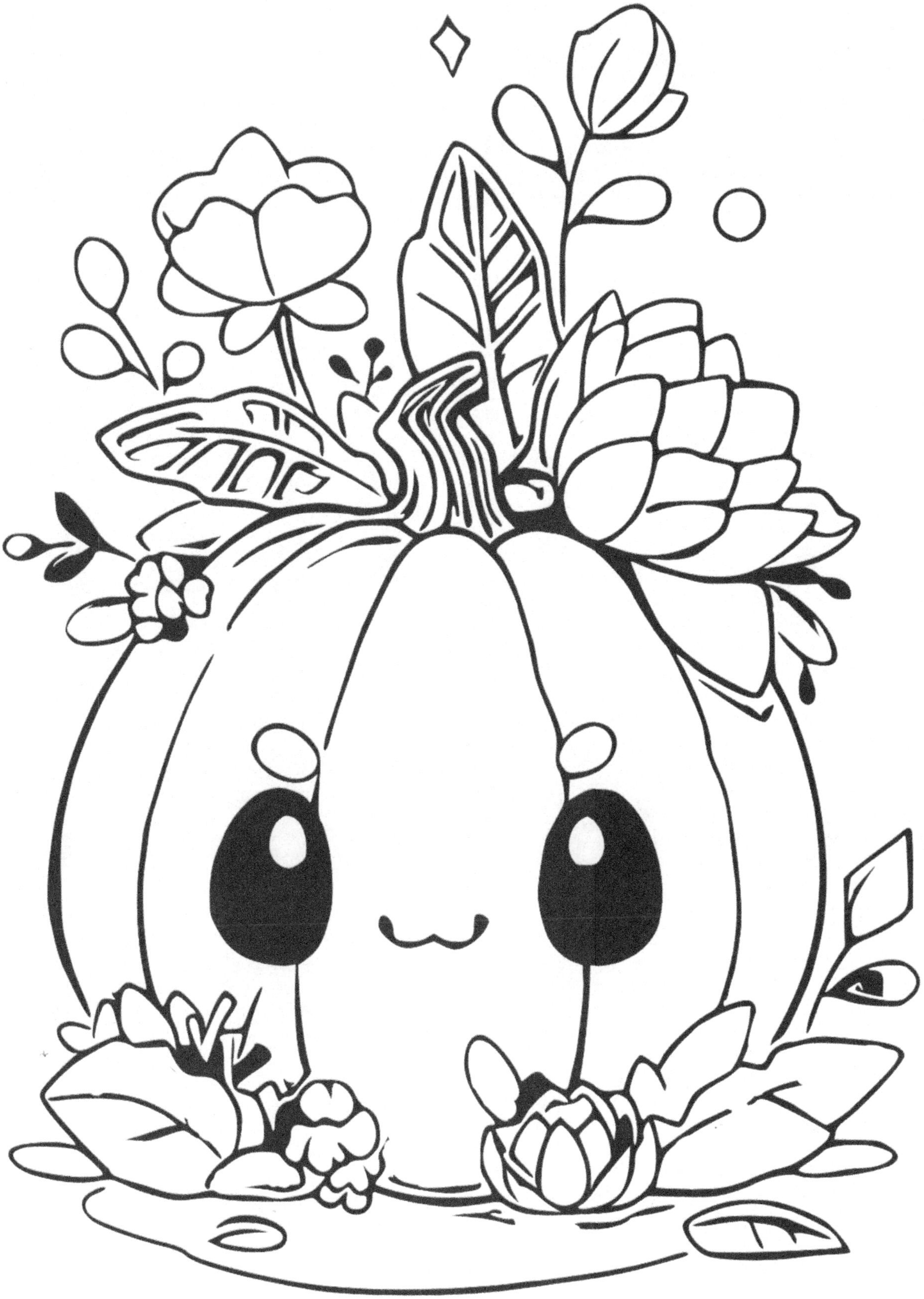

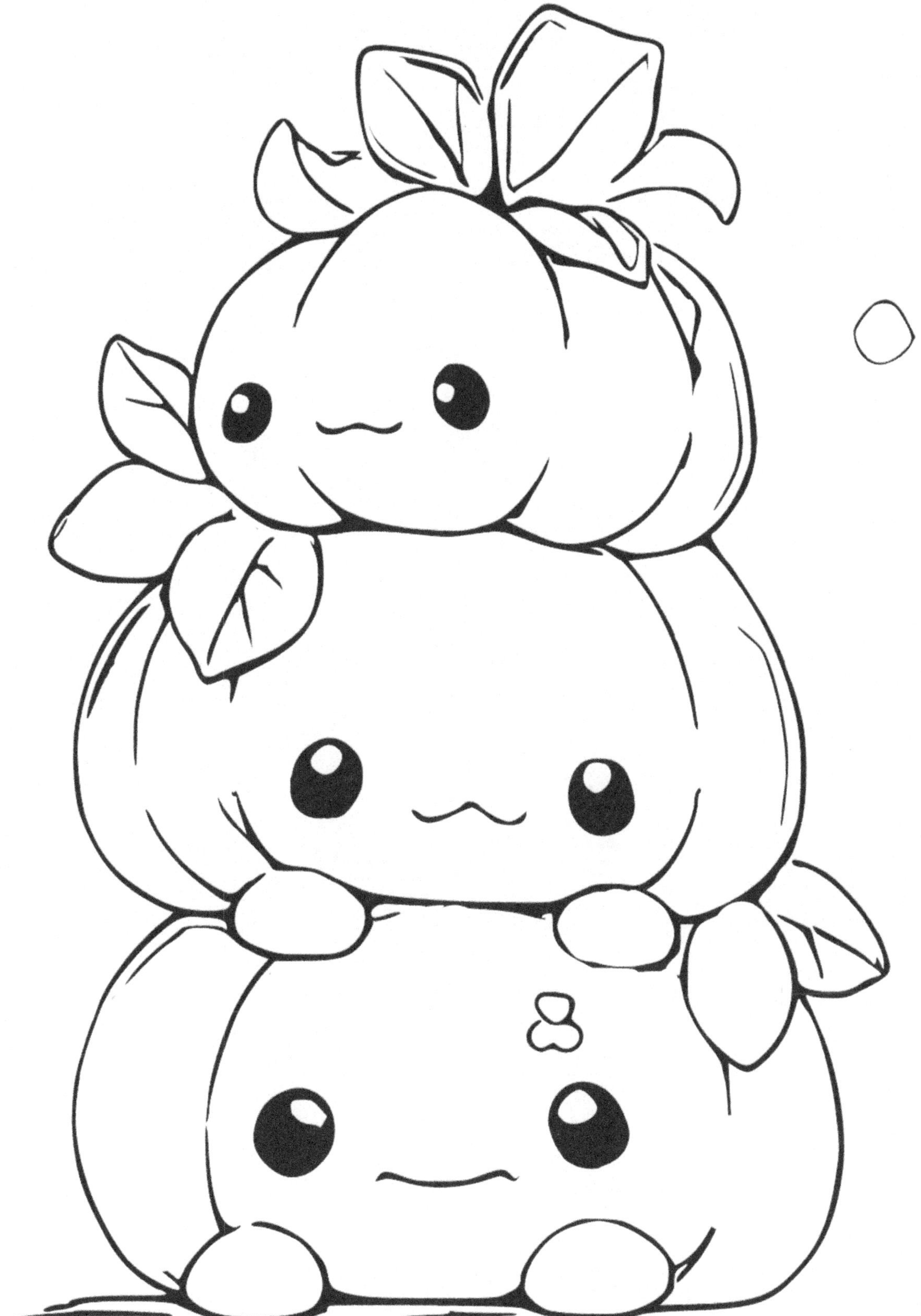

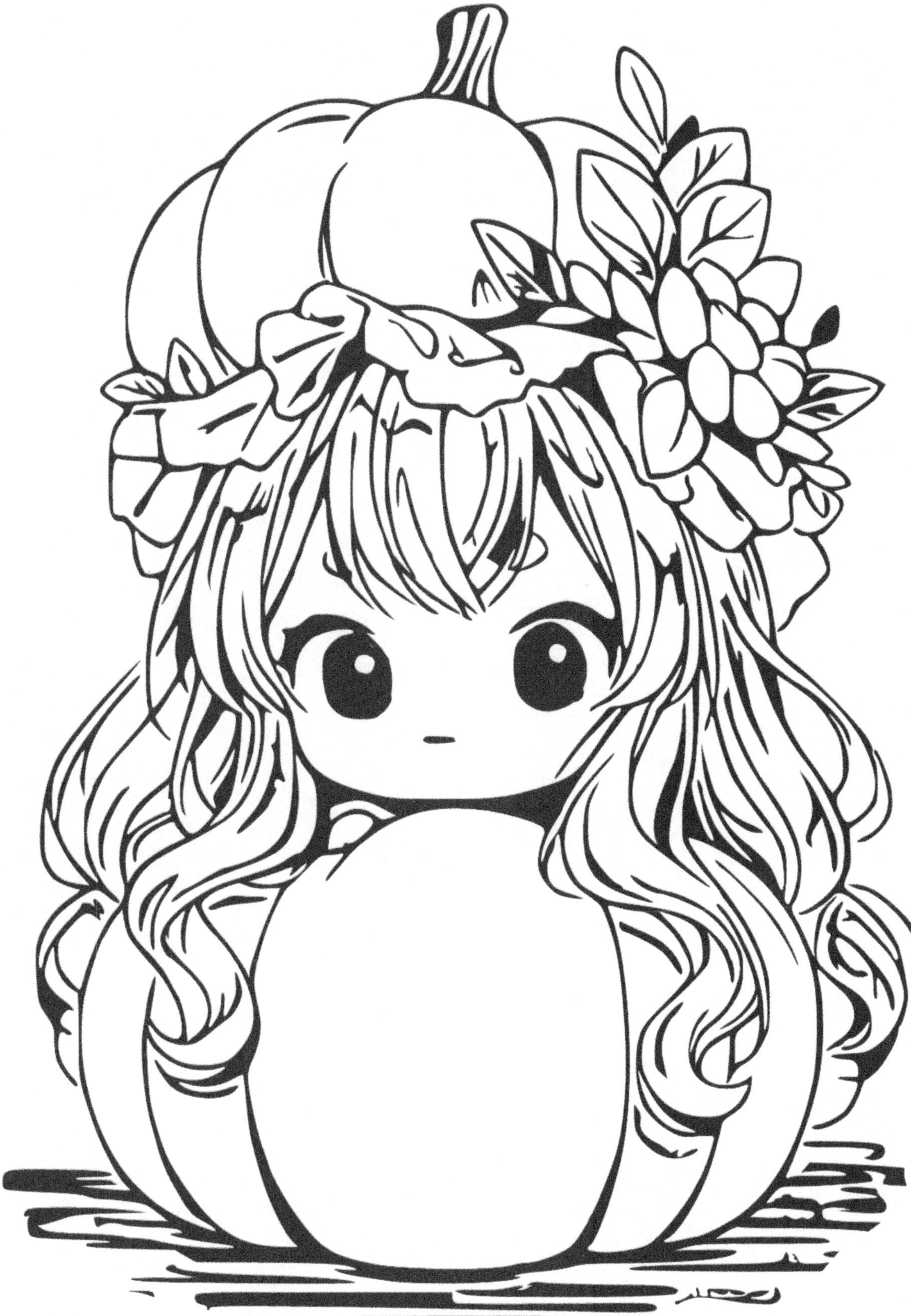

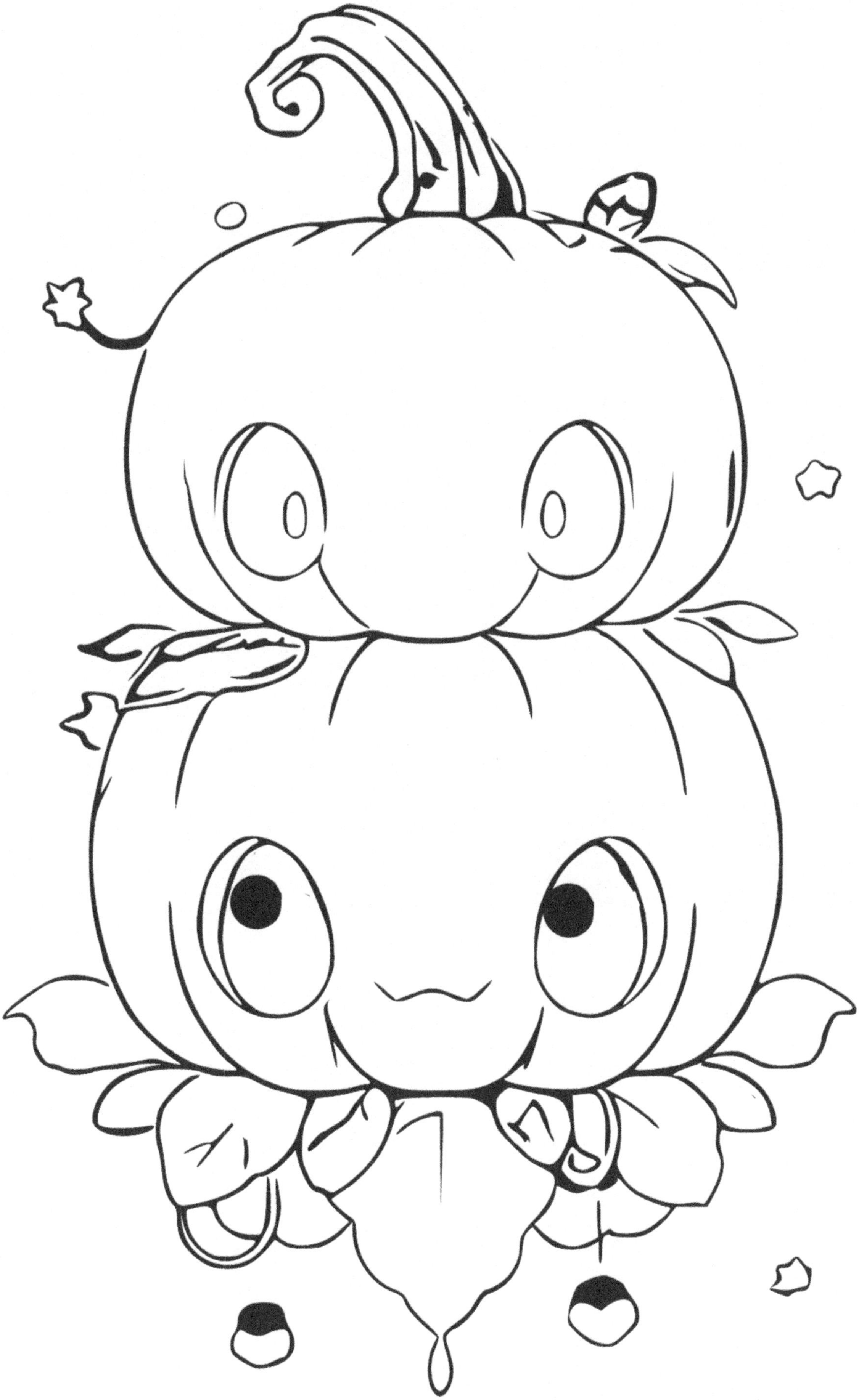

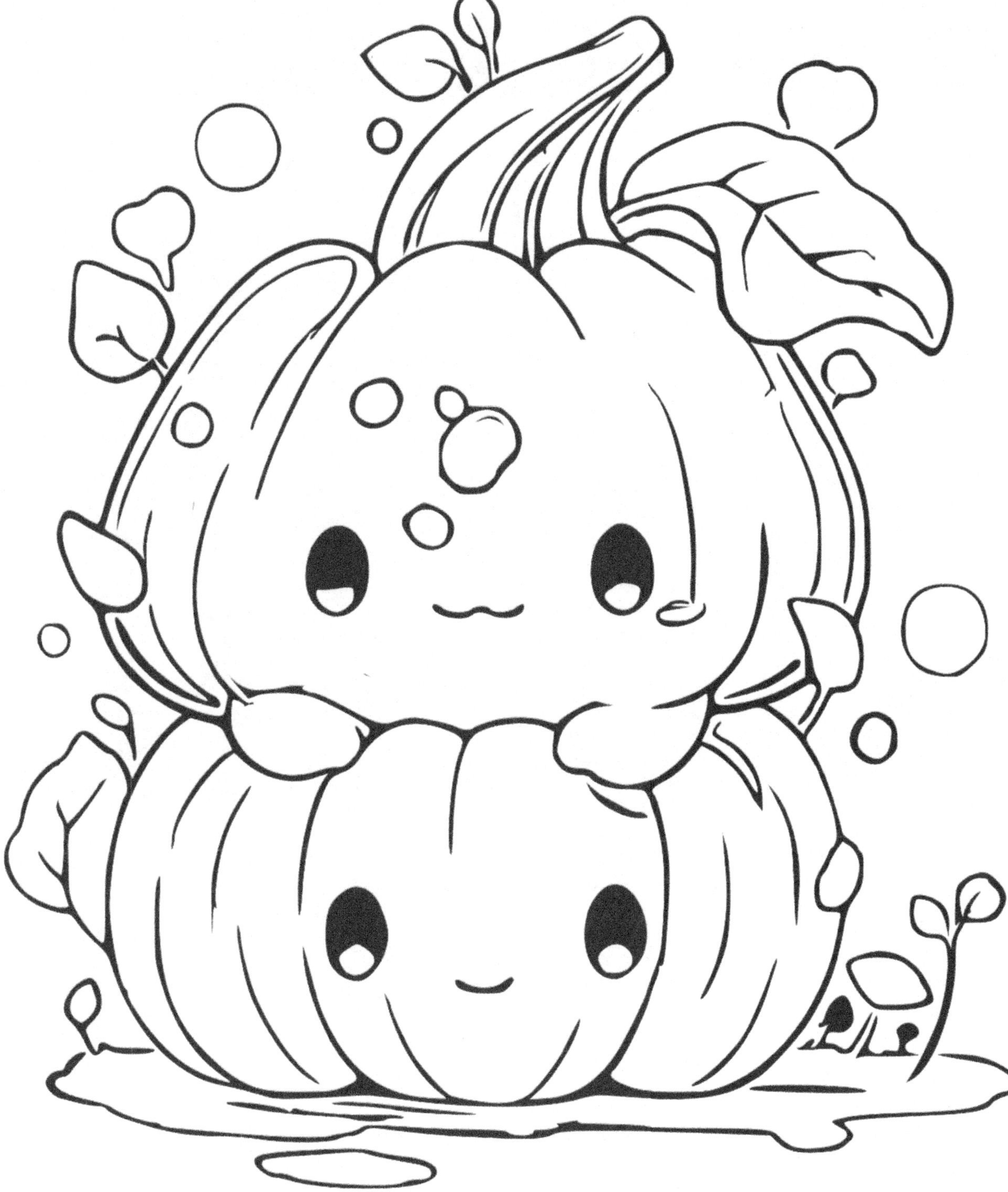

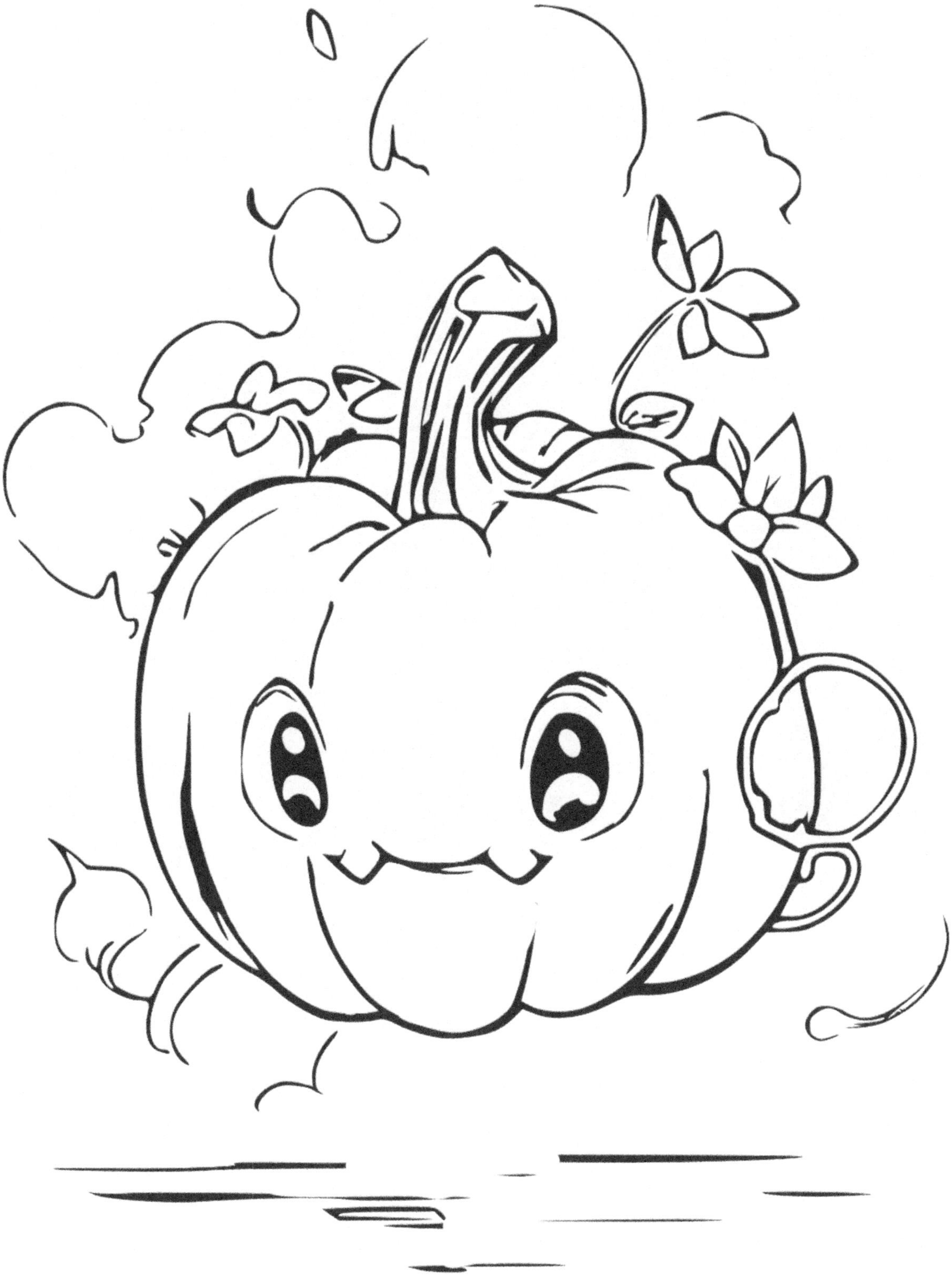

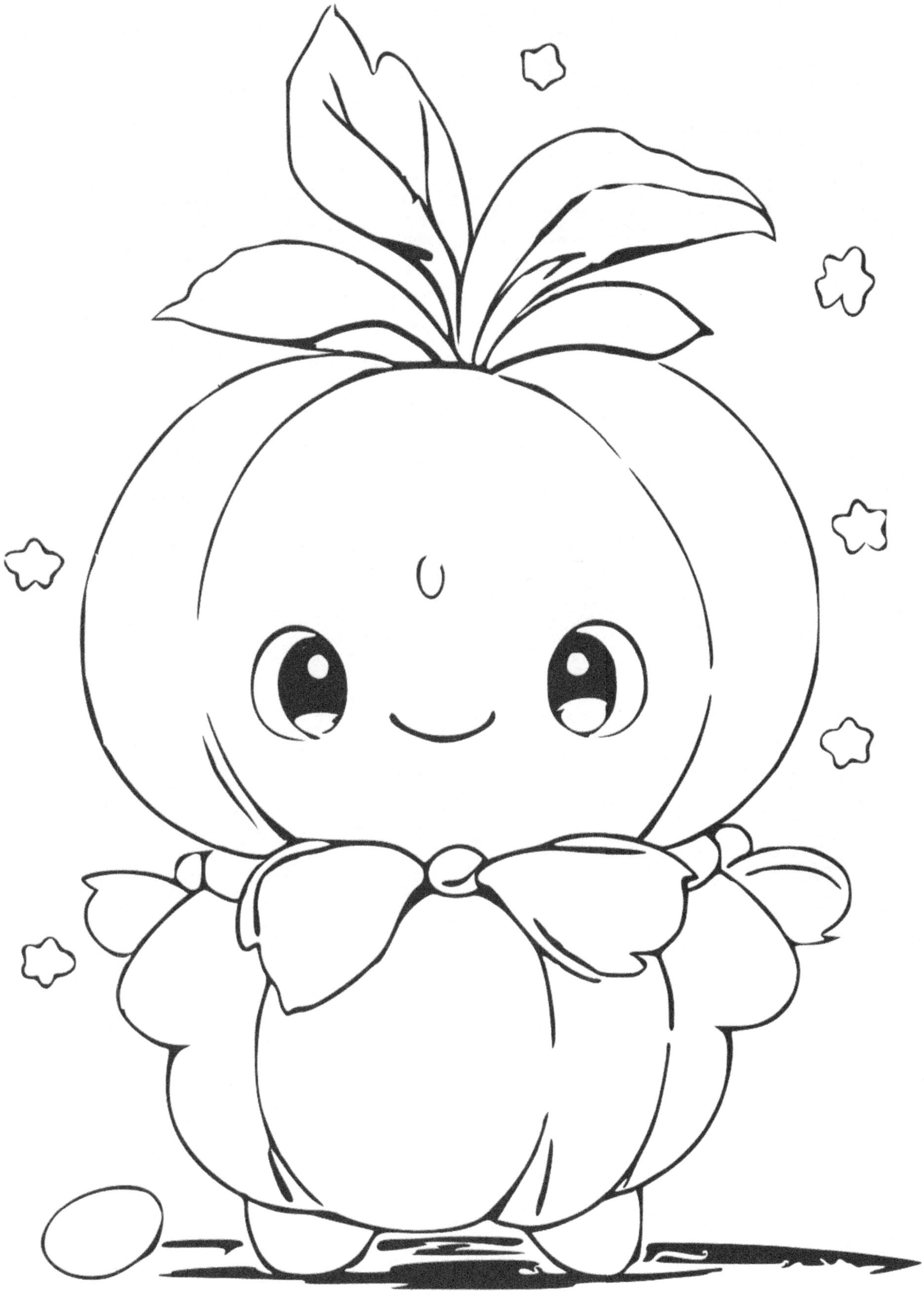

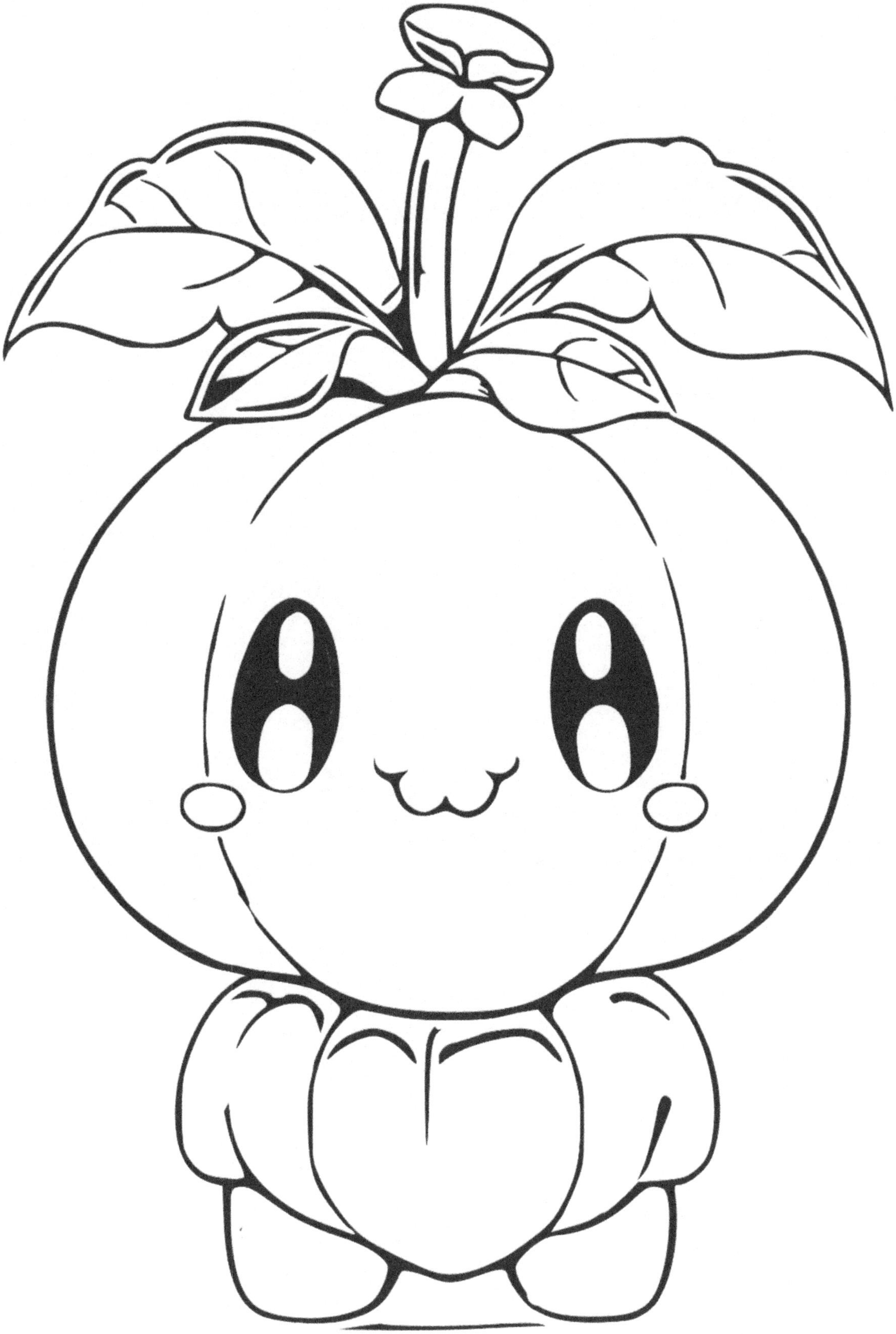

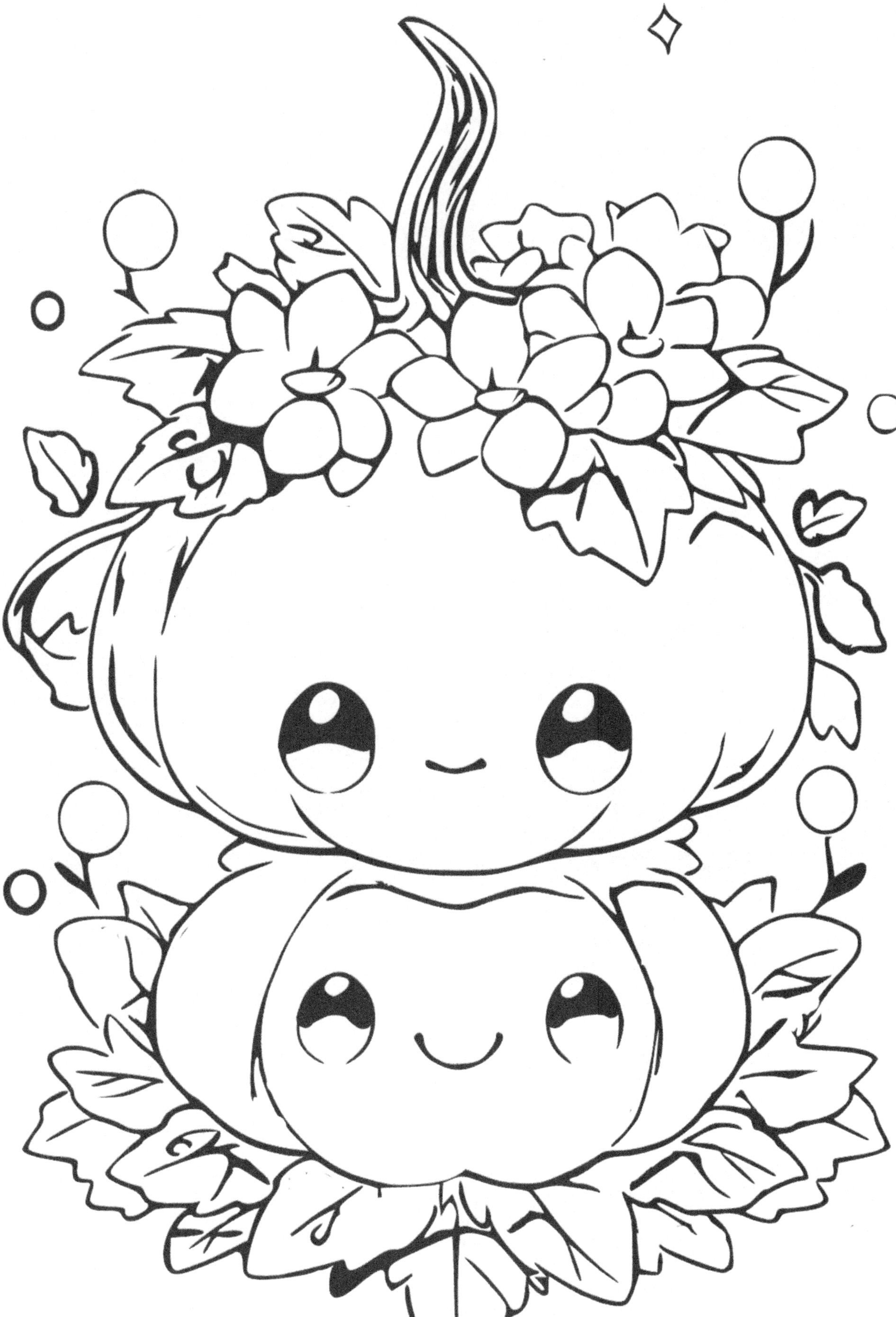

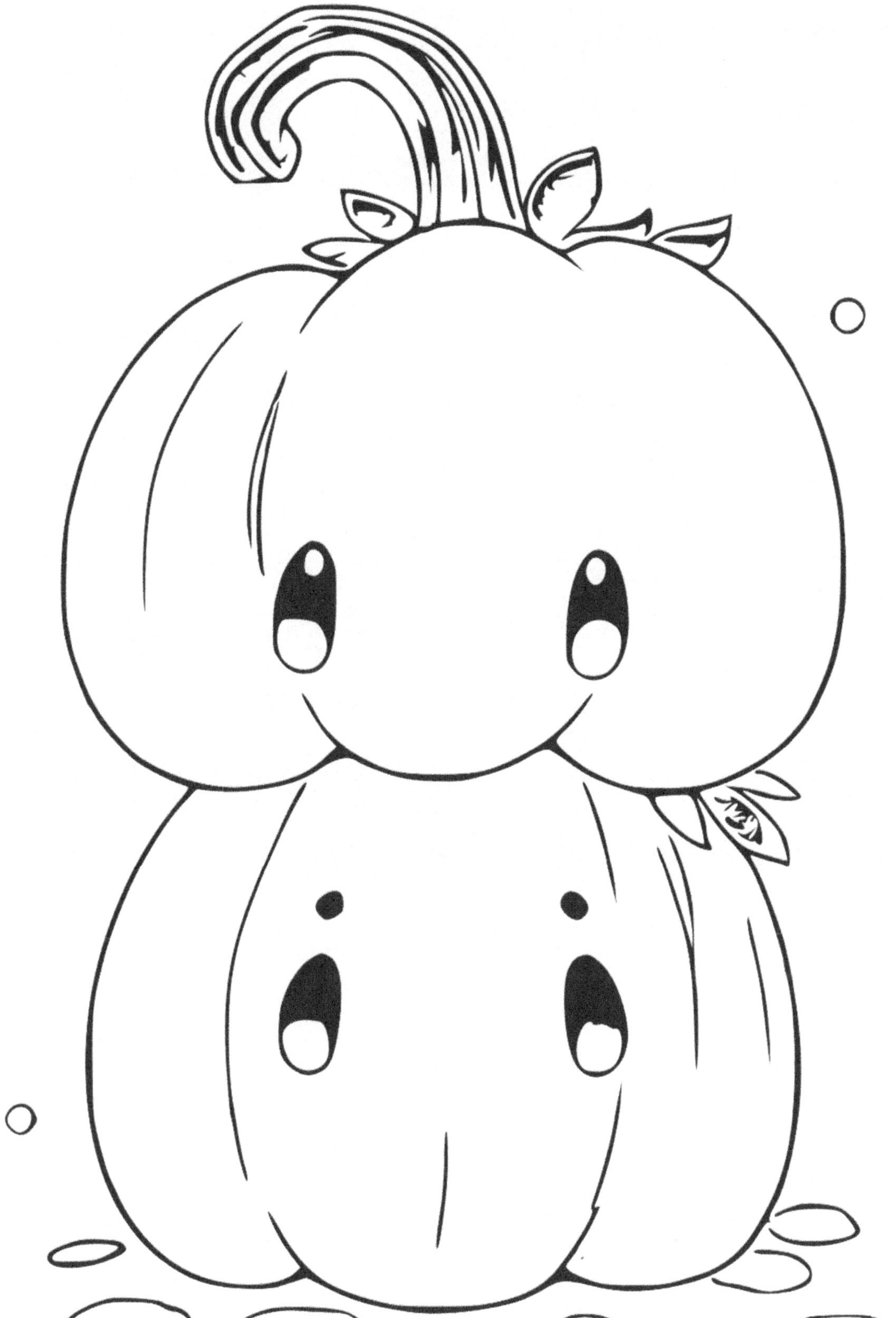

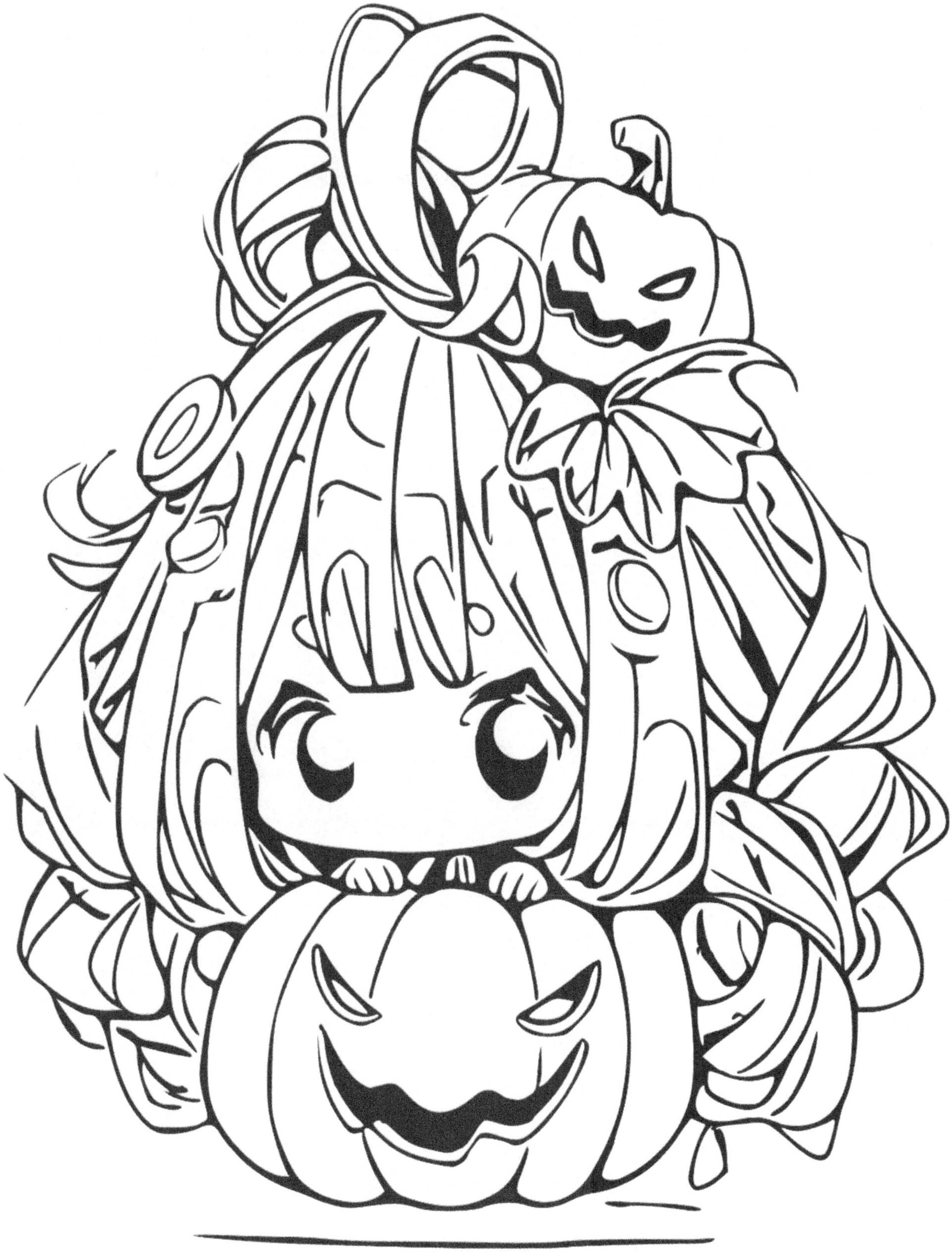

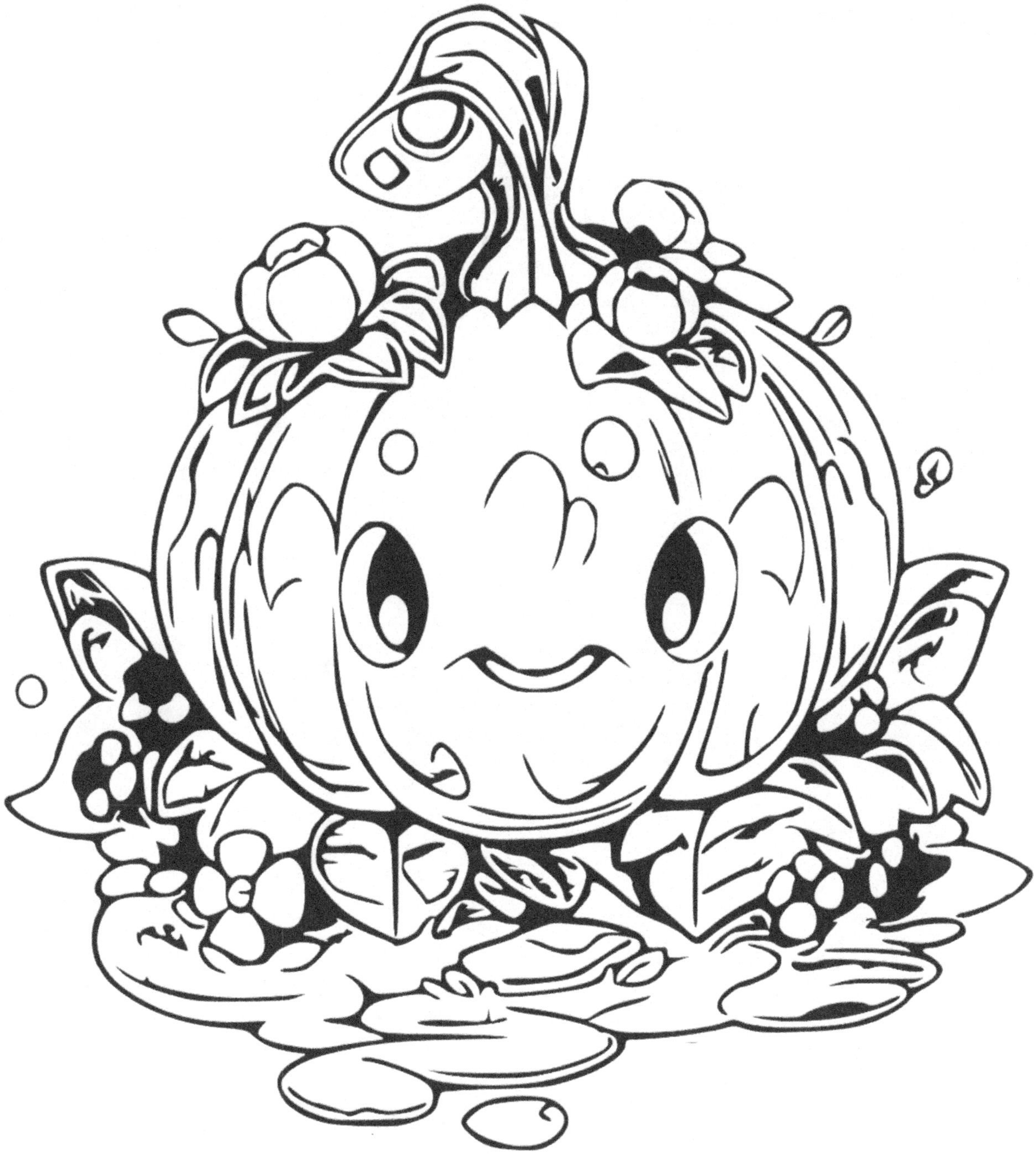

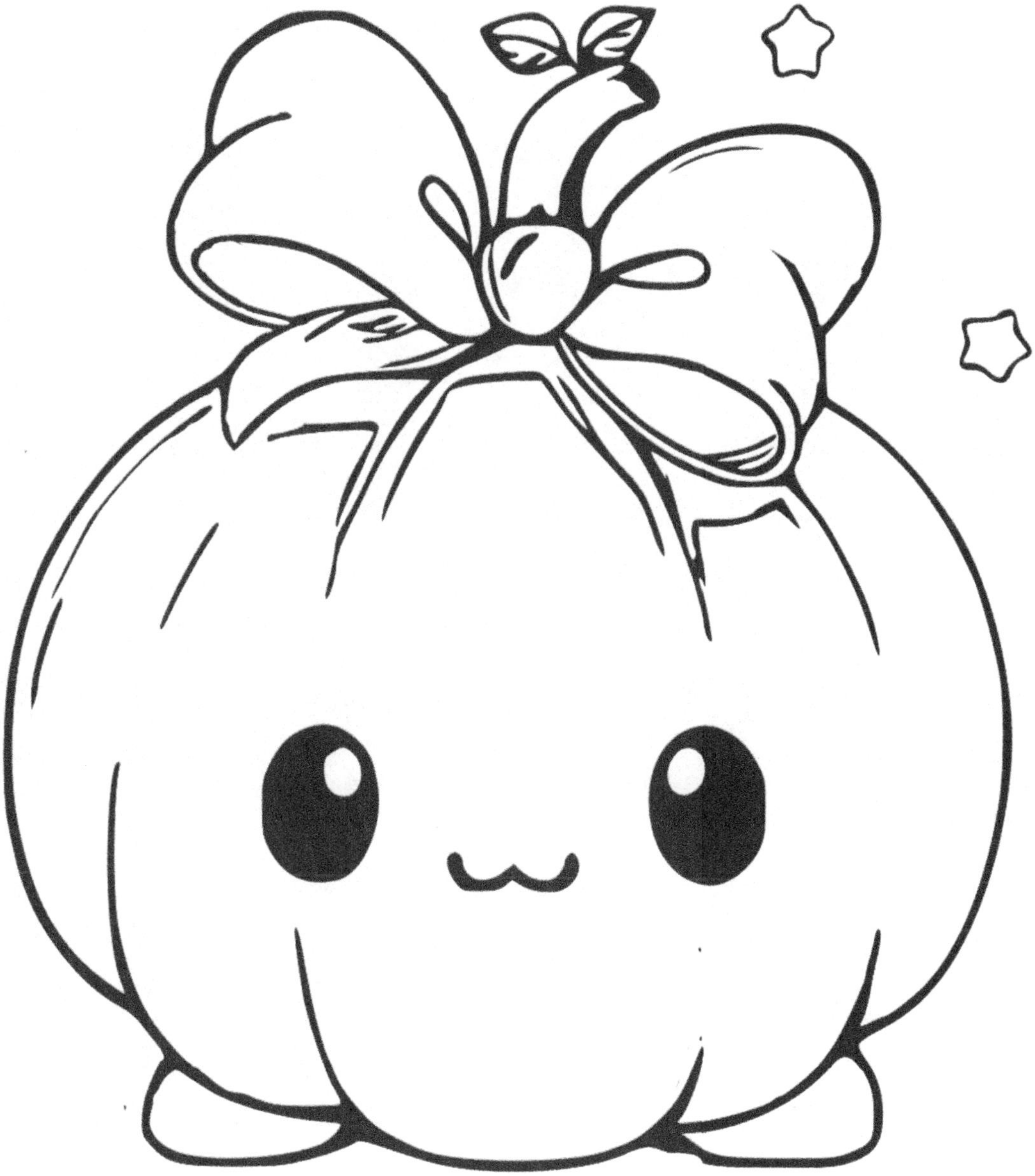

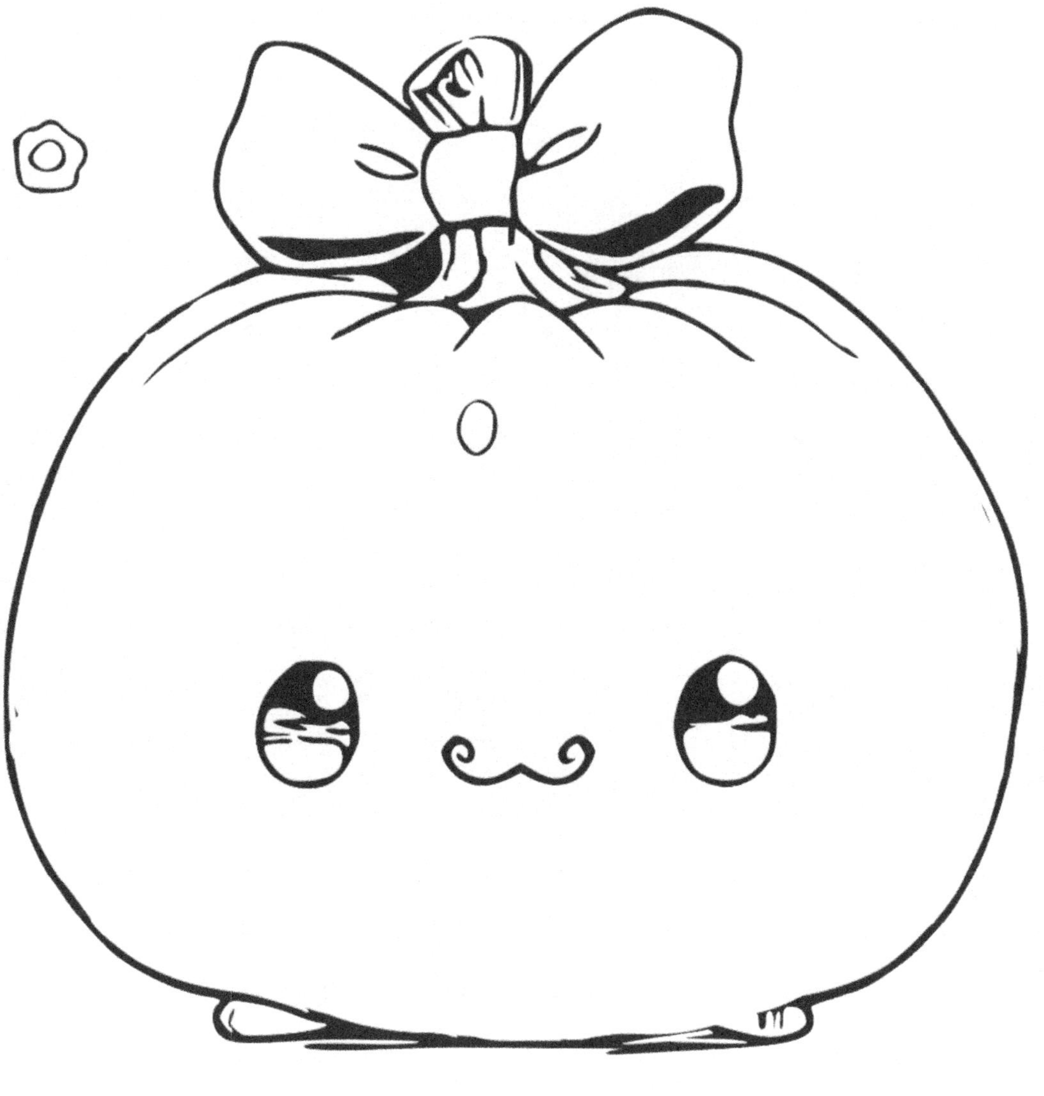

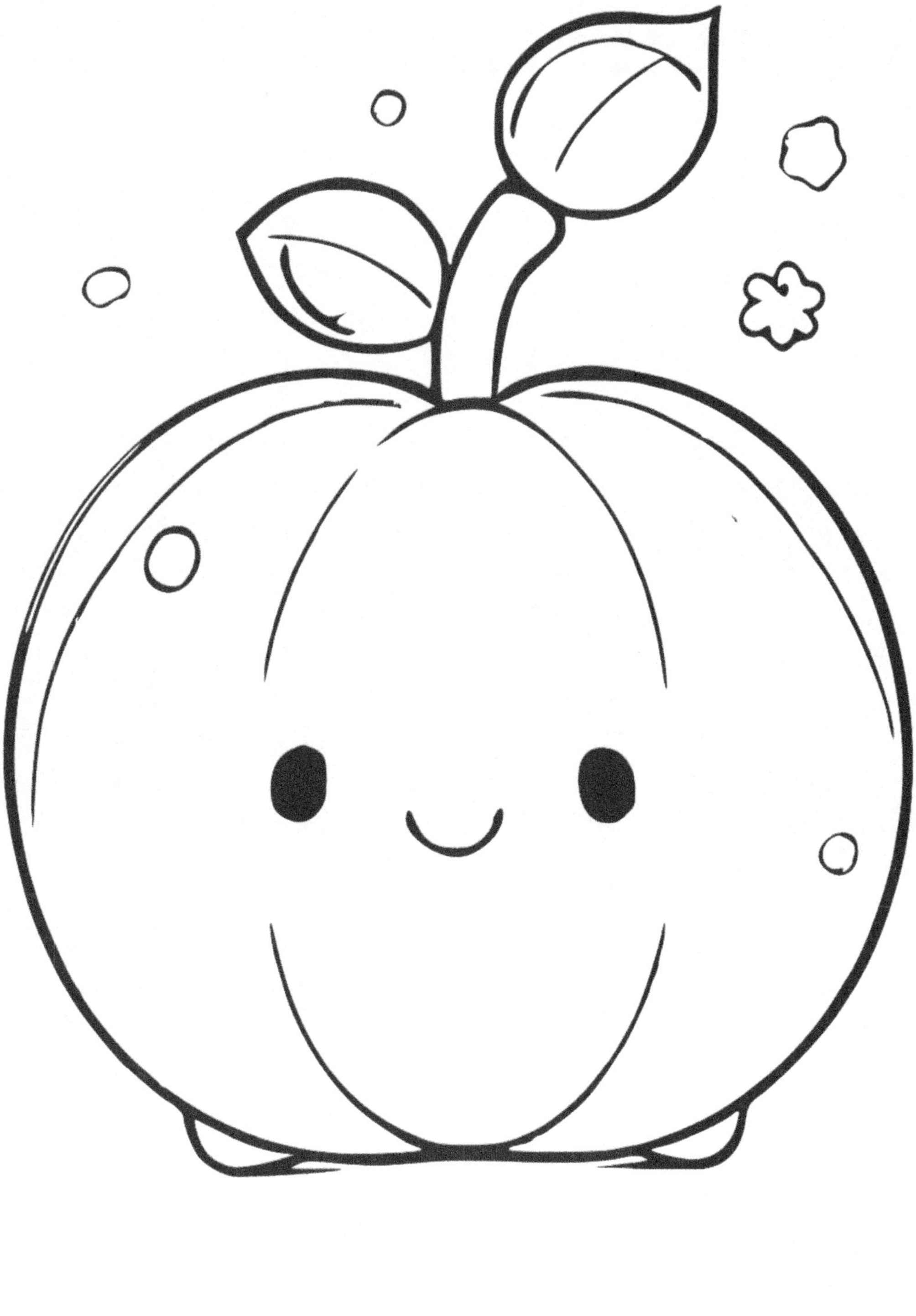

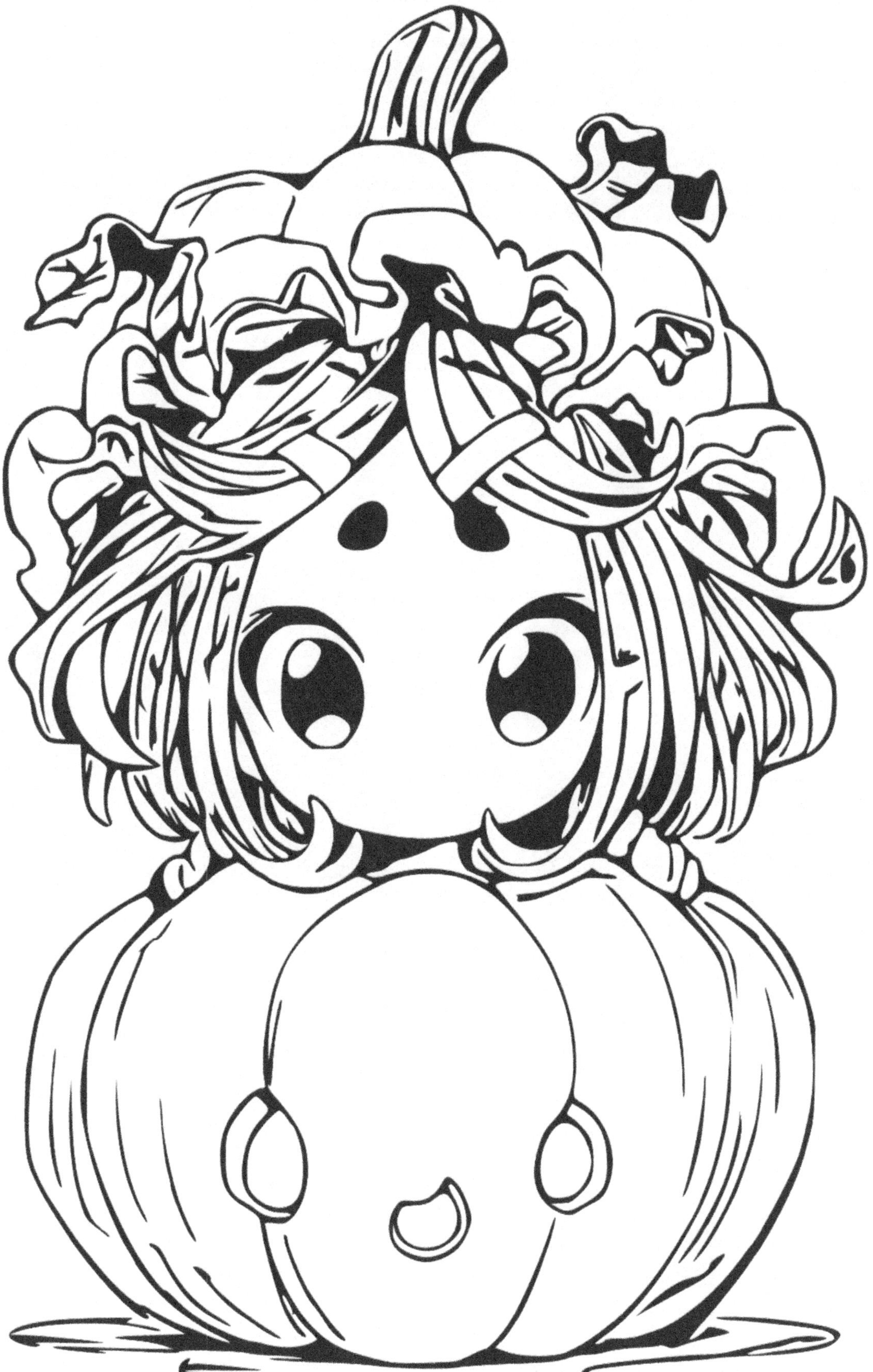

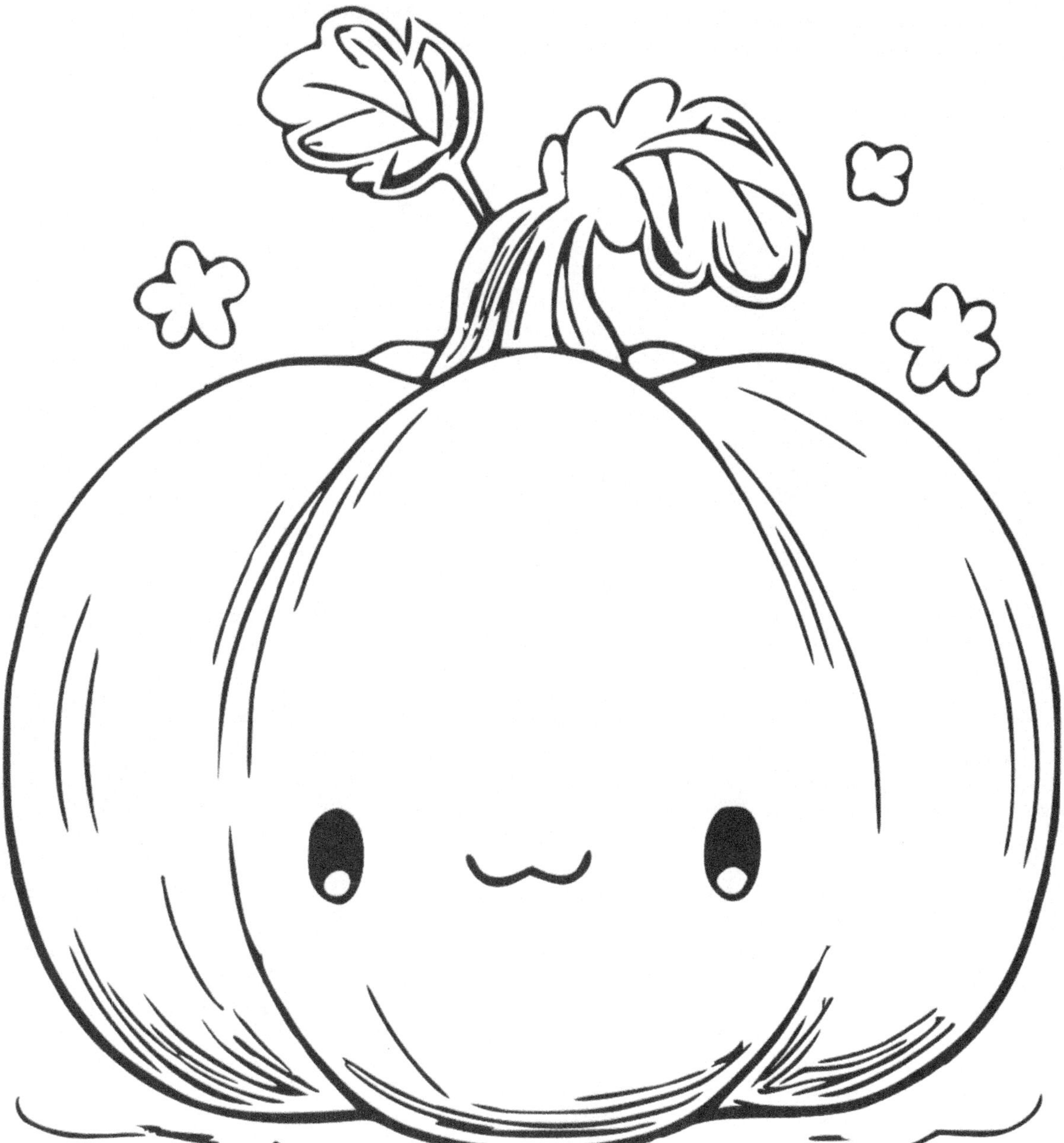

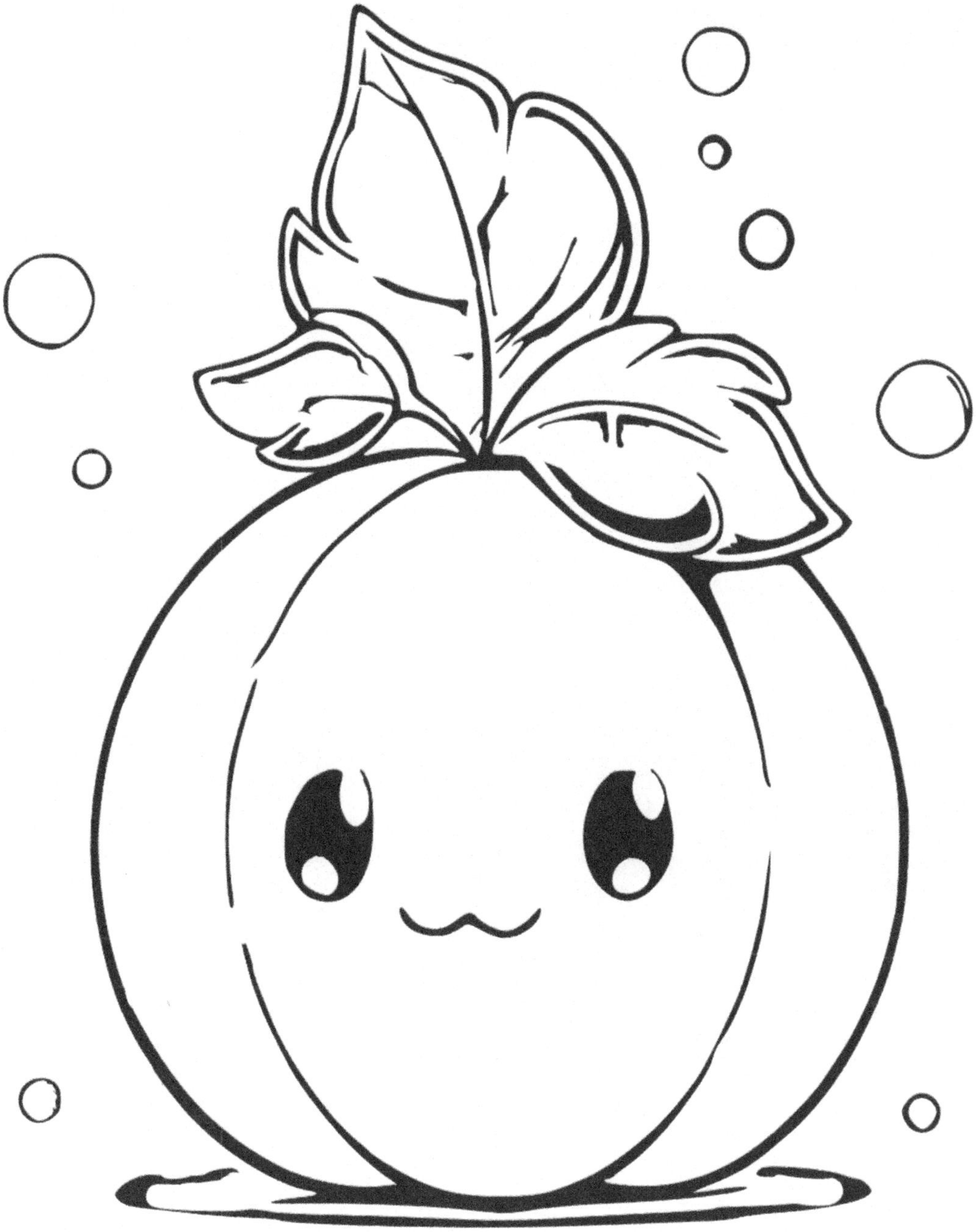

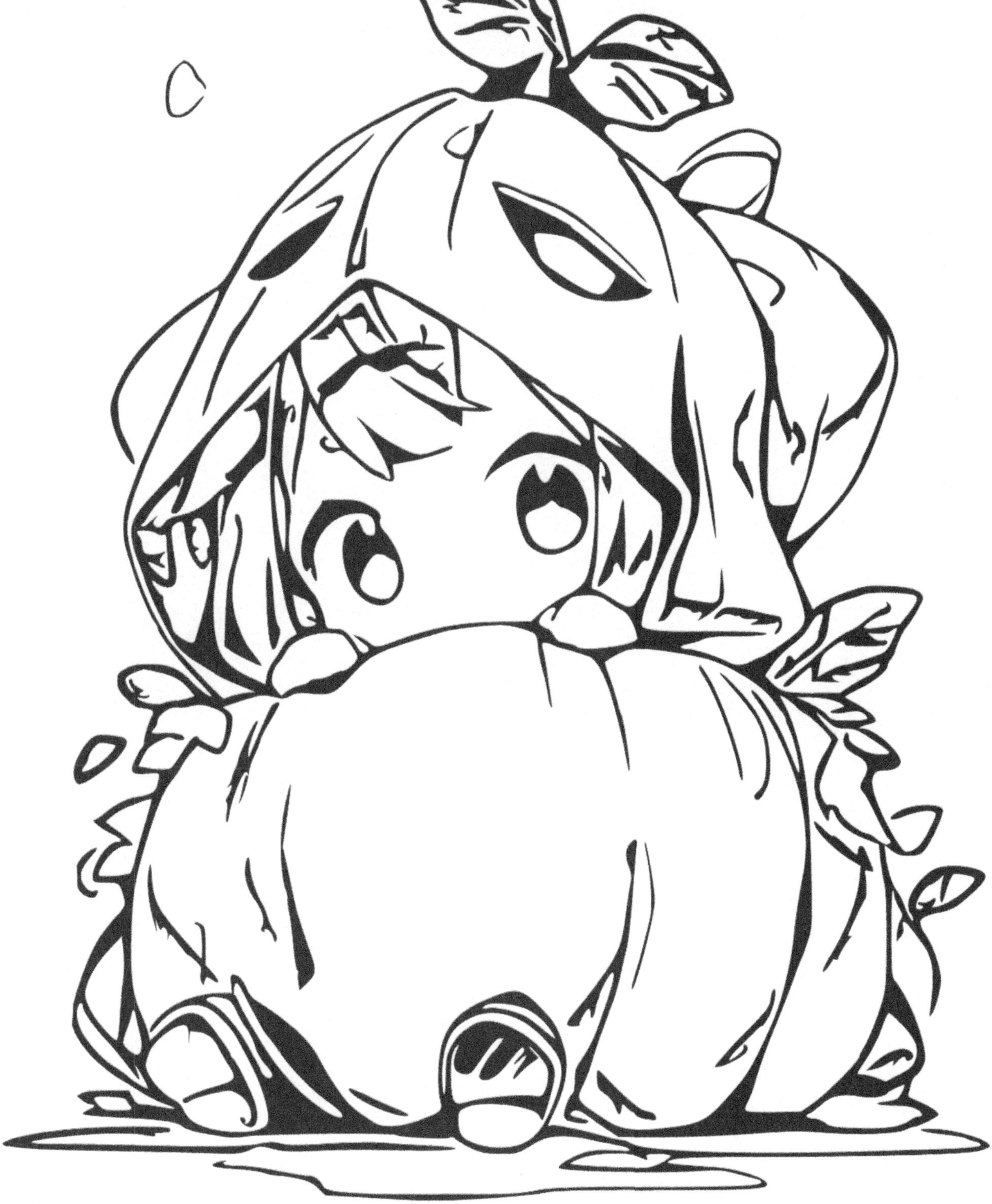

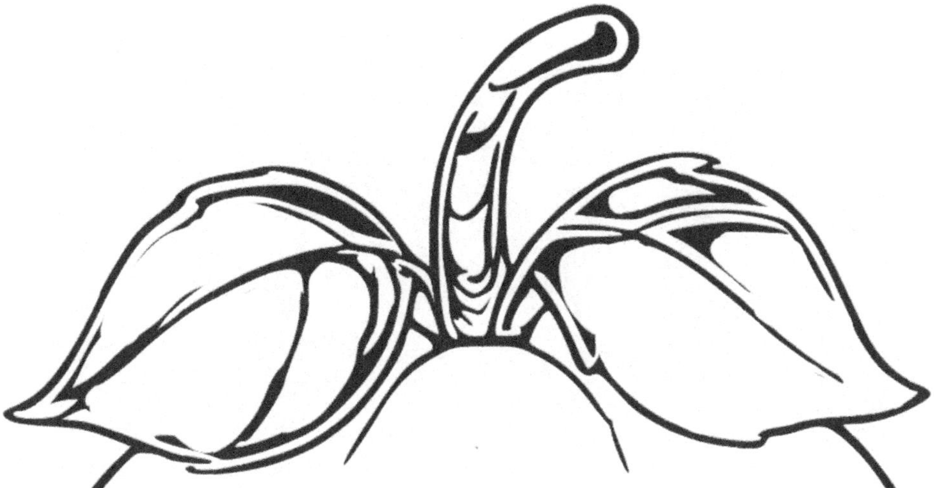

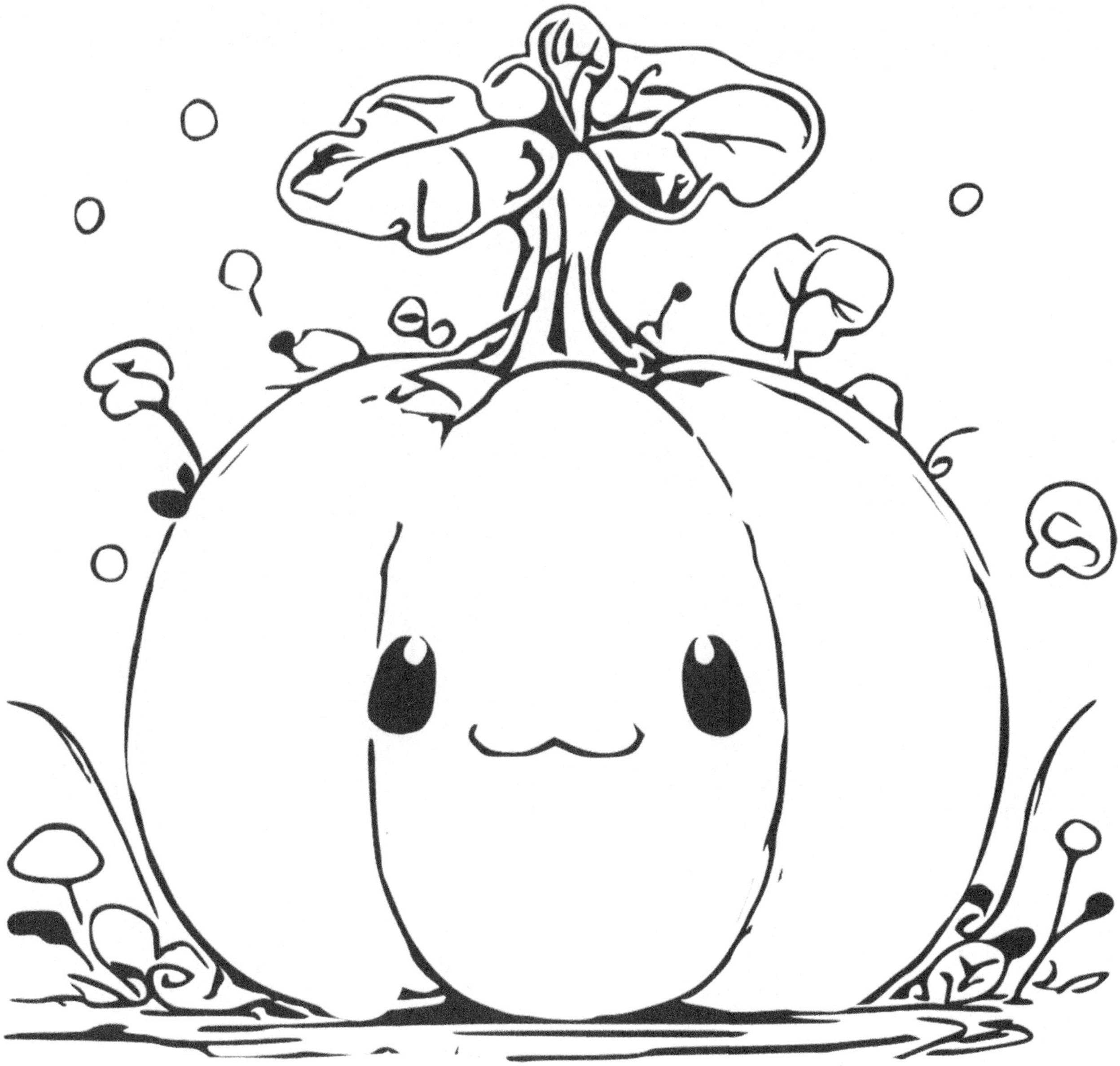

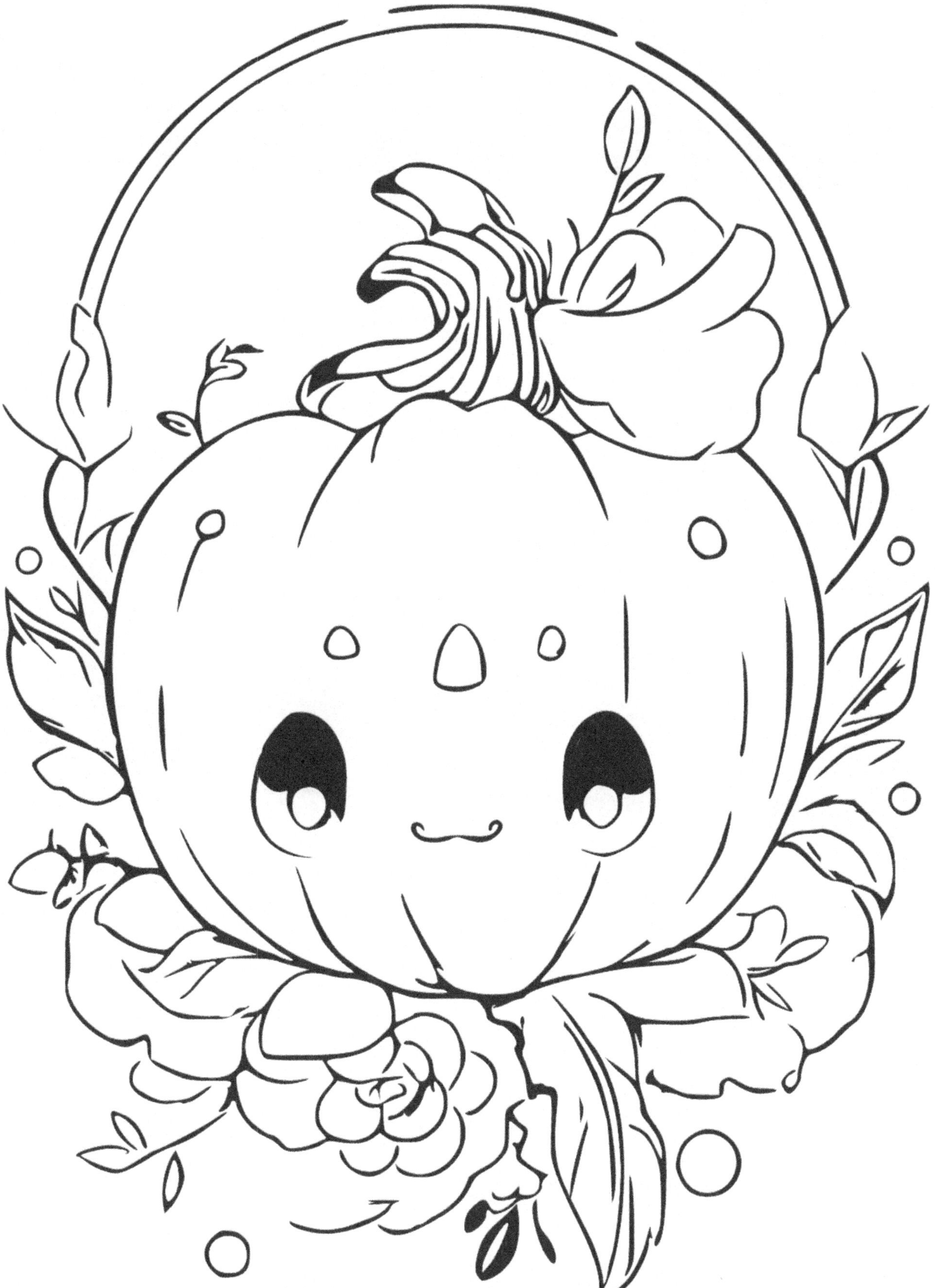

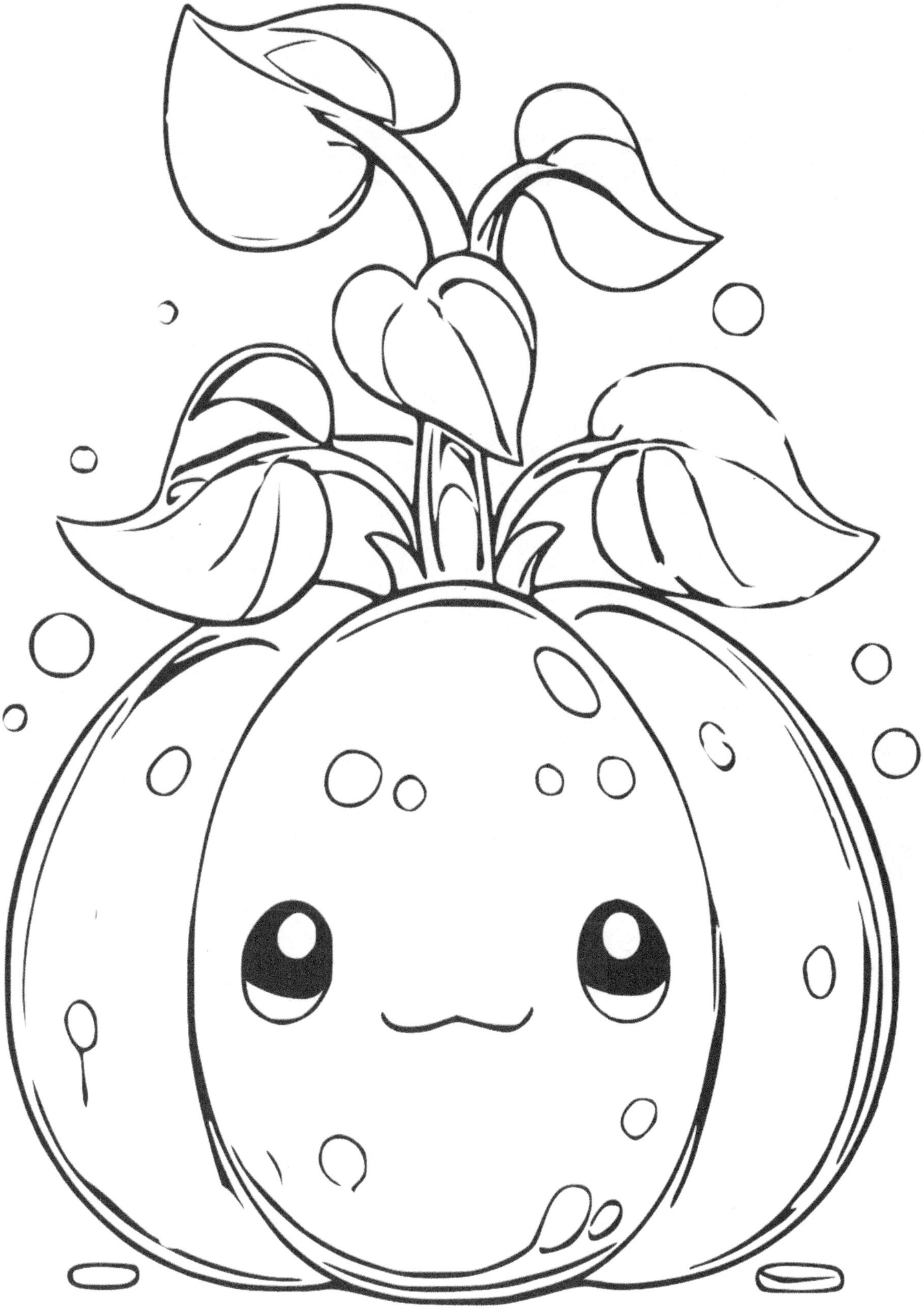

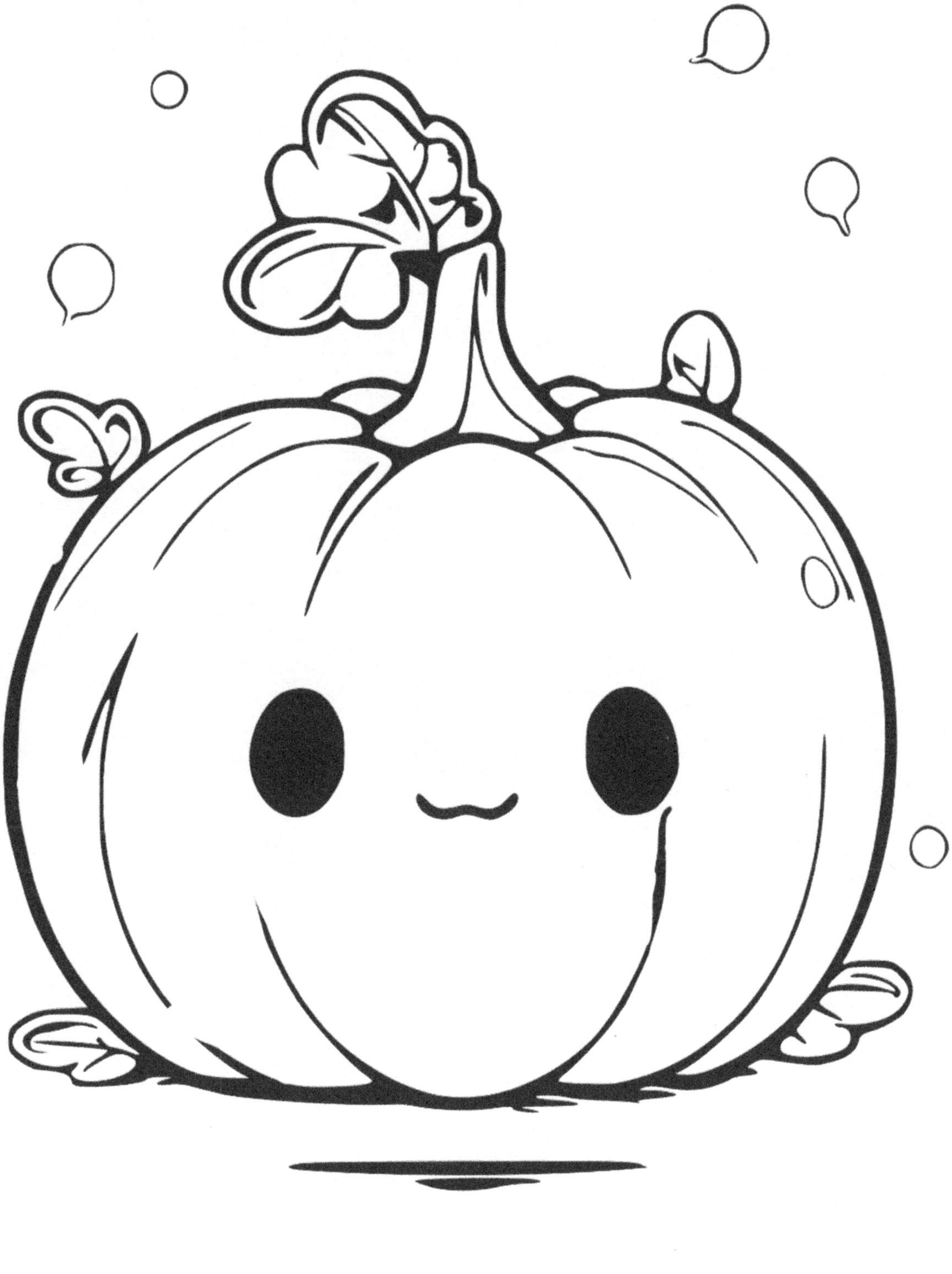

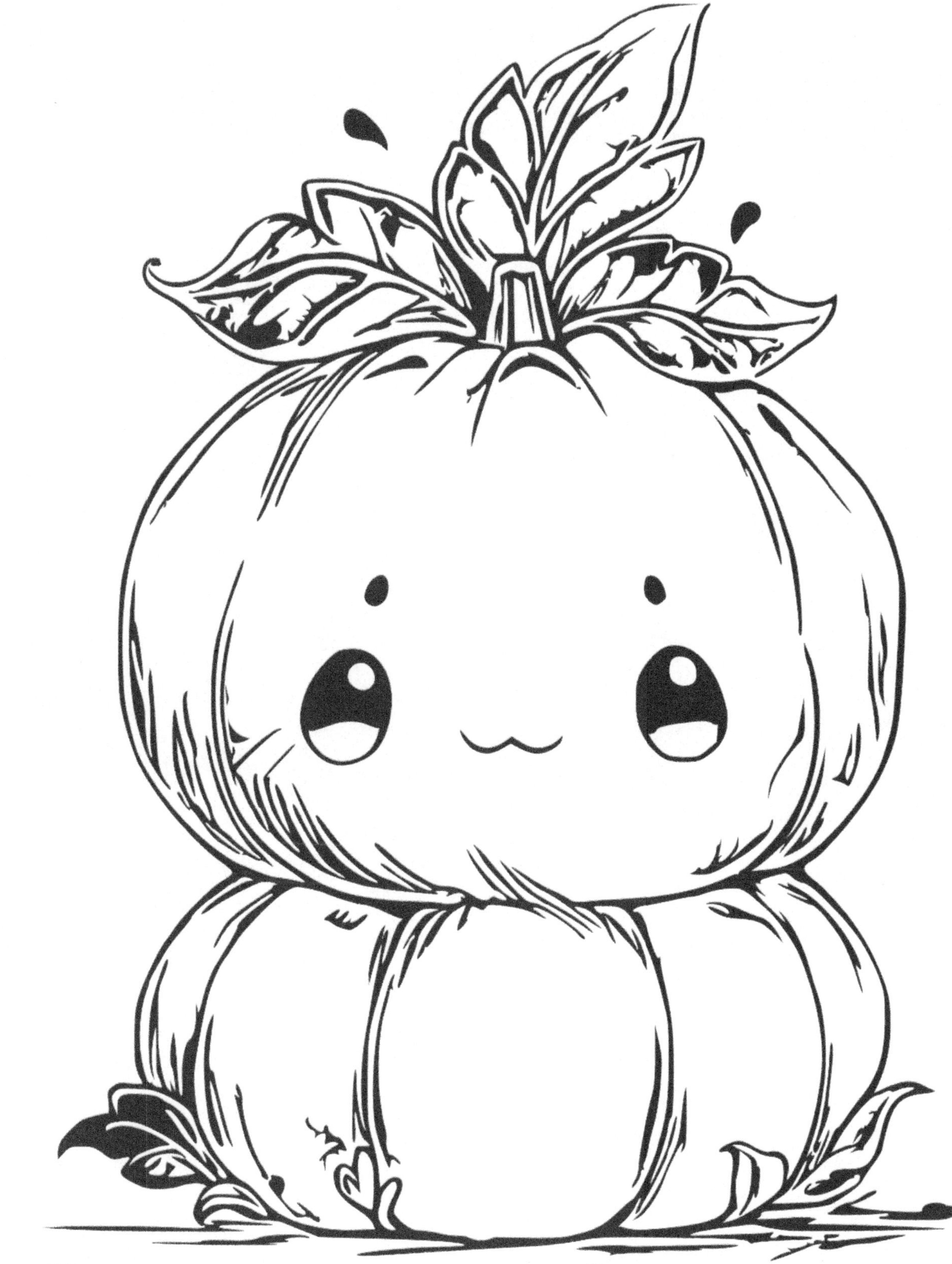

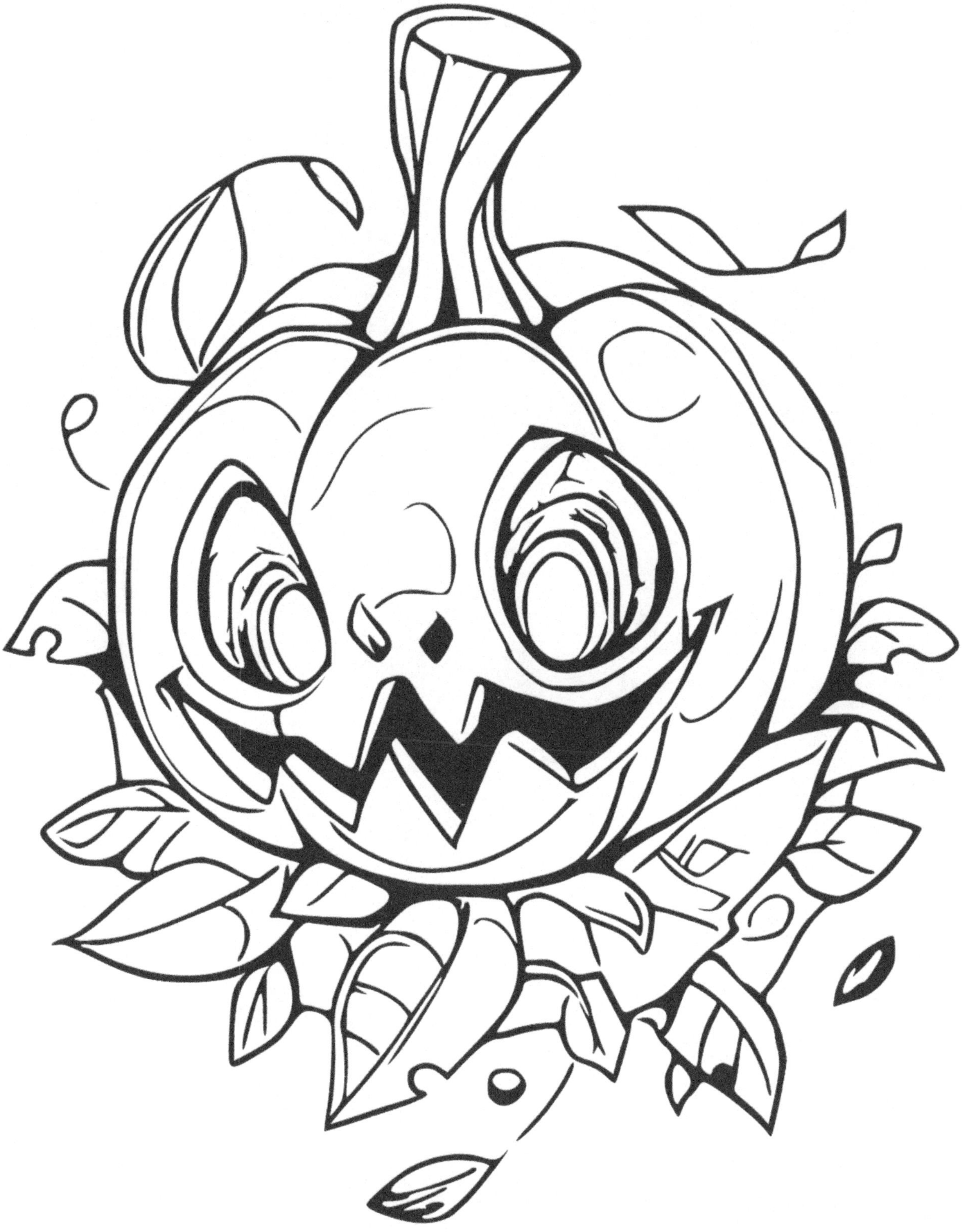

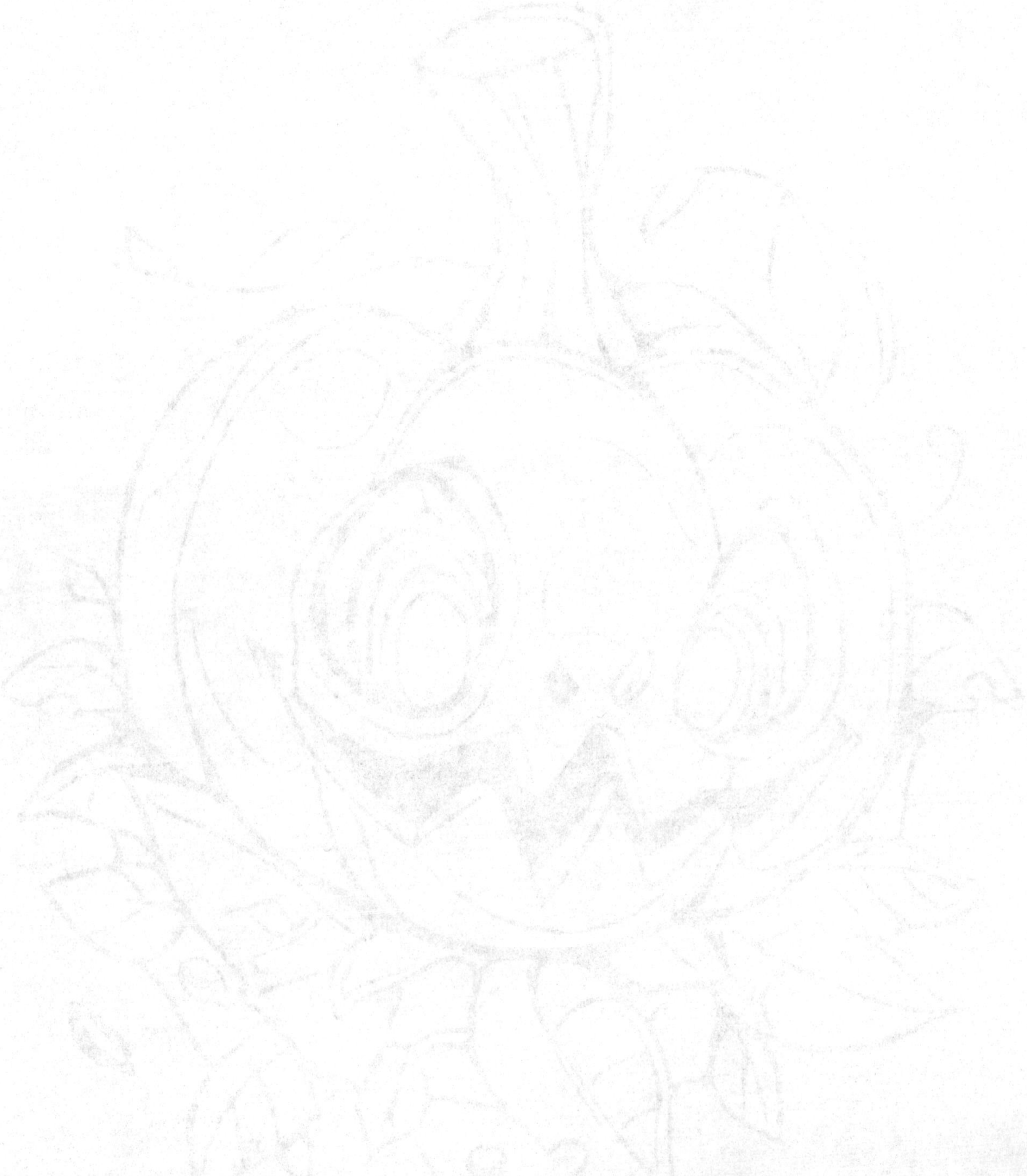

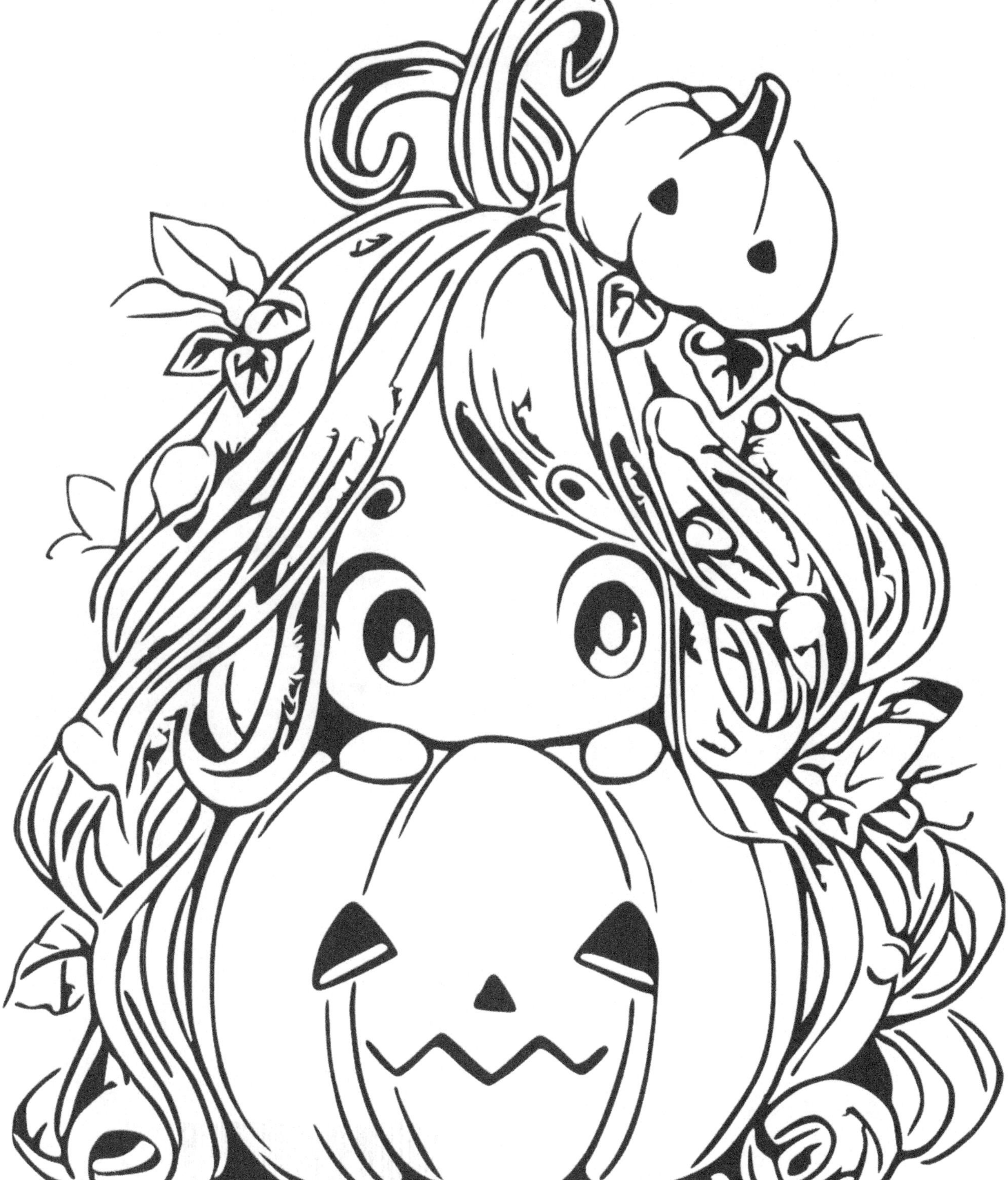

Made in the USA
Las Vegas, NV
29 August 2023

76785098R00057